A Pas Vision:

Th Story of Irma Stern

BY KATHERINE GRAHAM

Illustrated by Suné Raubenheimer

A Passionate Vision: The Story of Irma Stern

Published by Ambleside™ Publishers

ISBN 978-0-6399058-4-6

For more information regarding permission, write to:
Ambleside™ Schools International of Southern Africa
37 Denver Road, Lansdowne, 7780, Western Cape, South Africa

Editor: Elaine Ridge
Book Design: Comfort Adeola
Cover Design: Rozlynn van Reenen

All historic photographs are courtesy of the National Library of South Africa, Cape Town.

Printed and bound in South Africa
Salty Print, 15 Durham Avenue, Salt River, Western Cape

CONTENTS

Acknowledgements	iv
Chapter 1	1
Chapter 2	7
Chapter 3	11
Chapter 4	18
Chapter 5	24
Chapter 6	30
Chapter 7	37
Chapter 8	57
Chapter 9	66
Chapter 10	72
Bibliography	87
About This Book	88

IRMA STERN AS A YOUNG ARTIST PHOTOGRAPHED IN HER GARDEN AT THE FIRS

ACKNOWLEDGEMENTS

The author wishes to thank the following individuals for their contribution to this book: Susan Keegan for her vision; Mary van Blommestein, Kathy Wheeler and Christopher Peter of the UCT Irma Stern Museum for their encouragement and assistance; Laddy McKechnie of the National Library of South Africa for his tireless help; and Elaine Ridge, for giving of her time so generously to edit this book.

CHAPTER 1

Suné Raubenheimer

A general dealer's store like the one Irma's father owned, 1900

Irmakind, where shall we go today, London, Paris, Einbeck or where?" asked Irma's mother. All of the family, Father, Mother, Rudi and Irma were astride their black horses, ready for their regular Saturday morning ride in the veld near their farm house in Schweizer-Reneke.

Irma probably revelled in hearing her mother talking about cities in England, France and Germany that she had never seen. But even as a child, Irma was setting her sights on a life bigger than the one she knew: a life that spanned Europe and Africa, with Africa always first in her heart and in her art.

Little did she know she was to become one of the most famous of South African artists. Her exotic paintings vibrate with colour and emotion – the young women and men of Swaziland, the royal Watussi family in the Congo, the spice island of Zanzibar, the colourful fishing boats on the island of Madeira, Portugal. Although at first many South Africans rejected her art as ugly, by the time she died in 1966, she had already begun to enjoy the fame that was to make her one of the most celebrated artists of our time. Today her paintings fetch millions at international auctions.

The world that Irma Stern was born into in 1894 was very different from the world that you and I know. Schweizer-Reneke was the back of beyond; it was a tiny, dusty *dorpie* west of Johannesburg without a hint of sophistication. Electricity was not yet used in houses and there were no cars in Schweizer-Reneke, the small town where she grew up. Most people travelled on foot or on horseback. It was a farming community and most of the farmers who lived there were Afrikaans-speaking. The Transvaal – which covers the present-day area of Gauteng, Mpumalanga, North-West and Limpopo – was headed by the Boer leader, Paul Kruger.

Irma was not Afrikaans. Her parents were German. Her father Samuel ran the trading store that was the hub of the town. Farmers bought provisions and sold their produce there. You could buy anything from this store – vegetables and fruit, oil and flour, buttons and thread, paper and ink, wine and brandy – even a cow! There were only 150 people who lived in Schweizer-Reneke and Samuel and his brother Leopold Stern, who owned the store, knew most of them.

Schweizer-Reneke came into being only six years before Irma's birth. Before that, the area had been ruled by the Khoikhoi chief, David Massouw Taaibosch, who headed the Korana tribe.

The farmers attacked the stone fortress of the Korana whom they accused of stealing their cattle. A fierce battle was fought on Mamusa Hill in 1885. As a result, David Massouw Taaibosch and his people lost their land. Their settlement was replaced by the town of Schweizer-Reneke, named after two of the Boer captains who fought and were killed in the battle. But all that happened before Irma grew up. The Schweizer-Reneke she knew was happy and peaceful.

Irma loved to play in the veld surrounding her home, where she could watch the vervet monkeys, meerkats, baboons and springbok. She spent many hours sitting in the dust among the dry bushes, examining red grasshoppers as big as crabs, insects and butterflies of all shapes and sizes. Later this unspoilt African veld and the wild animals in it inspired her work as an artist.

As a child, Irma loved playing with big wax dolls with her best friends, Eva Einkammerer and Mandy Faustman. Eva's father owned the local hotel and Mandy was the daughter of the *dominee* of the local Dutch Reformed Church.

IRMA AS A BABY WITH HER NANNY

Irma's mother, Henny Fels, was from Einbeck, famous for its beer and quaint timber houses. Irma's father Samuel Stern came from the little town of Reichensachsen in Germany. His family were probably small farmers, cattle dealers and traders.

Irma wrote of her father: "Father is a so-called self-made man. He left the little town where he was born in order to seek his luck in America. After that hope was shattered, he came to Africa. There he worked himself up, returned to Germany and married my mother, an extremely young and very pretty girl with no fortune."

Both Irma's parents were Jewish and fairly well-educated. On 9 August 1883, when Henny had just turned 18, they were married in Einbeck. Writing about their marriage, Irma said: "It was from a sense of adventure rather than love that she married him – from a desire to escape from a restricted life."

There were certainly plenty of adventures awaiting the Stern family in Africa. Life was seldom dull.

The local farmers faced hardships resulting from drought, plagues of locusts and rinderpest, a disease which affected cattle. Despite this, Irma's family prospered. Her uncle Leopold was so well off that he could offer to lend money to the local Dutch Reformed Church. In 1918, he was the first person to buy a car in Schweizer-Reneke.

Even though Irma's parents were German, she mixed freely with the people in the town as a young child. Irma could speak Afrikaans and German, and could understand Zulu. She loved listening to the ancient stories the Korana domestic workers told her, such as the Jackal and the Sun Girl, which tells the story of how the jackal burnt his coat and got a stripe on his back.

IRMA WITH HER BROTHER RUDI AND HER MOTHER

Describing the house in which she was born, Irma wrote: "It was a very small house. Clay floors and a roof of corrugated iron hardly helped to make the rooms look better. It was called the 'white house', as it was painted white outside. Mother says it was cosy, although the rooms were small and there were a lot of ants in the walls. I can't remember it at all."

Later on, the family moved to a more spacious home in Schweizer-Reneke which had been newly built for them. Irma remembered the sun beating down on the white roof. "On the *stoep* covered with ivy and delightful blue flowers, it is refreshingly cool," she wrote in her journal as a teenager. "In the rooms the glare of the sun doesn't penetrate either."

There were many other Jewish people who lived in South African *dorpies* like Schweizer-Reneke at that time. The main reason that they came to South Africa was to escape persecution in Eastern Europe, where many people hated Jews and drove them out of their villages. Another reason was the opportunity created by the discovery of gold and diamonds in South Africa.

Just before Irma turned five, her brother Rudi was born. At about the same time, she contracted ophthalmia which made her eyes sore and swollen.

> *I was confined to my room by the Egyptian eye disease. For weeks I lay there in great pain. It felt as though fiery stones were burning into my eyes. It was a time of darkness and sadness – the doctors muttered something about blindness if the condition of my eyes grew worse. Blindness – it smelt of impenetrable darkness. And I loved the sun and the blue sky so much and all the bright flowers!*

The thought of never seeing the beauty of God's creation again was too great for Irma to bear. She went on to write:

> *Before my diseased eyes, I suddenly saw a red, fiery lily trembling in the hot glow of the sun. I smelt its sweet, somewhat mystical fragrance ... I knelt down before its beauty, drinking in its fragrance and form, its wonderful colour. My entire soul was filled with its beauty.*
>
> *Very gently I bowed my head as one kisses something holy. Everything dissolved before my eyes. I was intoxicated with beauty, with fragrance and with sunlight. I closed my eyes in enchantment.*

Fortunately, Irma recovered fully from the eye disease.

This was also the year the Second Anglo Boer War broke out. Irma described her introduction to it: "One day I went to play with Eva. Suddenly I stood enveloped in clouds of dust with a crowd of mounted men around me. I sat down and waited for them to pass. I was so frightened. They were soldiers. The Boer War had begun."

The war was fought between the British army and the two Boer republics between 1899 and 1902. For Irma, it meant that many of the farmers in Schweizer-Reneke were away on commando. The people in the town and surrounding areas feared that the Korana would seize the opportunity to revolt. Irma remembered going to bed fully clothed in case there was an attack and she and her family needed to escape in the middle of the night.

It was a difficult time for the Sterns. Irma's father Samuel and her uncle Leopold were arrested when Schweizer-Reneke was occupied by the British army. Accused of being Boer sympathisers, Samuel and Leopold were imprisoned in Vryburg.

Henny, Irma and her little brother Rudi left their home in Schweizer-Reneke for Cape Town. They lived there in some comfort for a few months. Irma remembered a home filled with toys and a double-storey dolls' house.

Here Irma went to play school and fell in love with drawing. "In Cape Town I began to colour pictures with coloured pencils. All the picture books were coloured in – all the children got red cheeks and blue eyes, my first attempts at painting."

In early 1901, Samuel and Leopold Stern were freed from prison. They had to sign a document saying they submitted to the authority of the crown (the king of England) in order to be released. The year was a significant one for Irma: it was the first time she travelled on a ship to visit the country of her parents' birth – Germany.

CHAPTER 2

Suné Raubenheimer

Berlin, 1909

In early 1901 the Stern family set sail for Germany on the Kinfauns Castle ship. In Hanover, Irma was warmly received by her aunts Grete and Erna and their families. She was wearing a white fur coat and looked adorable. Her Germany family called her "Little Polar Bear". To Irma's great amusement, there were two family members with the name of Fritz.

The home that the Sterns moved into in Berlin was in the Tauentzienstrasse, a fashionable street in the inner city where a number of artists lived.

Her education had thus far been neglected, but now Irma had to go to school. "For the first time I put on boots, brown-laced boots and didn't know how I was to get them off again," she remembered.

Her experience with German schools was painful. "At school I understand nothing at all," she wrote in her journal. At home her mother had to go over everything again. She remembered having at least 24 mistakes on every page of her school work. "Everything was terribly difficult for me." For a carefree seven-year-old farm girl, fitting into the routine and discipline of school life in a big city must have been hard.

In South Africa, Irma had spoken to her family in German, but she had not had any formal language lessons. Now that they were living in Berlin, her parents decided to employ a tutor called Fräulein Redel to help her. This tutor was a very devout Jew and "had a great influence on me," Irma wrote.

> *Formerly I had never wanted to be Jewish. Once I stayed behind sobbing all by myself in the middle of a wood because Aunt Grete had called me a little Jewish girl. Now I became terribly pious. At least, I believed I had, for I would only eat meat from kosher butchers and once Aunt Grete, with whom I was staying for a few days, discovered that I always tore off the toilet paper on Friday in order not to desecrate the Sabbath.*

Like many German Jews in the early 20th century, the Sterns were wealthy and saw themselves as part of the German Empire. Their Jewish heritage and religion was not as important to them as it had been to their parents. The Jews played a large role in many German enterprises, including banking, retail, trade, the arts and publishing. At the time, Berlin had a Jewish community of about 200 000 people.

Jews had been given full rights as citizens in the German Empire in 1871, but there was still a lot of ill-feeling against them in Germany. The Sterns mixed only with their relatives and other middle-class Jews. They saw themselves as different from the more religious and lower-class Eastern European Jews.

Irma's parents, like many other Jewish people, were not particularly concerned with Jewish law and practices. However, Irma's family still observed important festivals like Rosh Hashanah (the Jewish New Year) and Yom Kippur (the Day of Atonement). On these days, they did not work. Instead they went to the synagogue in the morning and in the evening.

Irma as a young girl in Germany

Berlin was not to be Irma's home for long. No sooner had she settled in Germany than her father announced that they were moving back to South Africa. The Second Anglo-Boer War had ended and Samuel was eager to return to his general dealership in the Transvaal.

Nothing could have prepared Irma for the sight of Schweizer-Reneke on her return. During the war, many of the farms in the area had been destroyed and women and children had been imprisoned in concentration camps. The area was a wasteland of burnt grass and farm houses. Only the shells of buildings remained, with many windows and doors missing. The smell of rotting dead animals filled the air.

The church, which had been used to house British soldiers, was still standing, but the parsonage had been completely destroyed.

In the first directory of the town to be published after the war, Irma's father Samuel was one of only two people listed among the white population. However, later editions added an assistant resident magistrate, a postmaster, a headmaster, two general agents, an auctioneer, a hotel and the firm of Stern & Co.

It must have seemed rather bleak, especially after the cosmopolitan charm of Berlin. But the Sterns showed how remarkably resilient and adaptable they were. Irma referred to her family at this time as "gypsies". After a year back in Schweizer-Reneke, they returned to Germany in 1904, via the east coast of Africa, Naples and Rome.

Again, the family lived in Berlin where they settled in their own home and went on holiday to Bavaria and Austria. When she was 12 years old, Irma had a childhood crush on Bernard Cahn, a German-American, whom she described as "a very sweet boy with black hair and wonderful dark eyes".

When she was 15, she was introduced to her new tutor who was to have a big impact on her life. "One day when I was just busy trying on clothes, I was called. In the smoking room sat my new tutor. The first thing I noticed was that he wore a watch chain and that he was grinning," she wrote in her diary.

In 1910 Irma's family had discussed getting a suitable governess for Irma, but in the end they decided to appoint the 25-year-old Dr Johannes Prinz instead. Their choice of male tutor was strange. He had obtained a doctorate in philosophy from the University of Munich the previous year, so was hugely over-qualified.

Why someone with his background – he was also a member of the Lutheran Church – would have been prepared to teach the 15-year-old daughter of a Jewish shopkeeper in a remote South African village is a mystery. Perhaps Prinz had a sense of adventure, for he accompanied the Stern family on many of their travels between Europe and South Africa.

No longer a child, Irma was beginning a new phase. She was slowly becoming more aware of the beauty of the world around her and her desire to capture it through her art.

CHAPTER 3

Suné Raubenheimer

The Carlton Hotel in Eloff Street, Johannesburg, 1910

In 1909, the Sterns returned to South Africa. This time it was just a short visit – only a year. Instead of living in Schweizer-Reneke, they chose to settle in Wolmaransstad, 120km to the east, where Irma's father started a new store.

Wolmaranstad was also a small town, about the same size as Schweizer-Reneke, but with a slightly larger population. There was a Dutch Reformed Church, a hotel, a doctor, three stores, an undertaking business, a bank, two butcheries and a post cart which carried the mail to and from Klerksdorp twice a week.

From 25 December 1909, Irma began a diary which she kept on and off for four years. On the first page she wrote, *Tagebuch* (Diary), probably adding *aus meiner Sturm- und Drangeszeit* (the storms and dramas of my life) at a later stage. In this journal she poured out her heart, sharing all her inner thoughts and the ups and downs of her daily life as a teenager. Some of it was written in code so that prying eyes would not be able to understand it.

This was her first diary entry:

> *It is now Christmas Day, it's hot and oppressive. In the house it's unpleasant for there's thunder in the air, indoors as well. Father, Uncle Walter and Grandfather, who came out to Africa with us this time, are having business problems and arguments. Aunt Erna has been ill, she had stomach cramps and got up again for the first time. Mother has a lot to do, mainly because it's Christmas and we're expecting visitors for Boxing Day (Hettie, Fritz and Mrs Sonnenberg are expected) and I'm helping her in the house. I hate being in the kitchen, I prefer sitting somewhere all day reading or drawing (I feel I have quite a gift for it, as all my teachers have told me so, as well as a painter who looked at my sketch book). I love riding and got a saddle as a present yesterday. I mostly ride Lichmann (my favourite horse).*

It was quite unusual that Irma's Jewish family celebrated Christmas, albeit very modestly. This was possibly because of Irma's Christian tutor, Dr Prinz (whom she affectionately called Doctor) and because all their neighbours would have been marking the festive season.

In the same diary entry, Irma recalled playing duets with her mother on the piano and singing Christmas carols. "We had no tree and only gave small presents," she said.

She remembered being moved by how gratefully the servants received their gifts: "It was so touching to see how happy they were on Boxing Day." She wrote that she was looking forward to spending New Year's Eve in Schweizer-Reneke, the place where she was born.

In the eyes of a teenager who loved theatre and dancing, Wolmaransstad could not measure up to the many attractions of Berlin. Nevertheless,

Irma's diary entries show that life in the town was surprisingly full of social activity. There were always people in the house, relatives and friends who came to stay, as well as ordinary visitors.

Social events at the time included a wedding and a dance which the Sterns gave. "It was great fun," Irma remembered. "From 10 o'clock till three in the morning." The family loved to spend time together at home, singing to the accompaniment of the guitar or playing tennis. They also liked to play practical jokes.

"It's been very pleasant and agreeable here again lately," Irma wrote in a diary entry in the winter of 1910. "Father and Mr Michaelis had driven out to some farm. We were all sitting close to the fire on the hearth. Doctor was playing the guitar and we were all singing. Then we made punch and the hot drink made us jolly and also a little tipsy, at any rate Aunt Erna. We danced, sang and made a lot of noise."

During this time, the Sterns made trips to the diamond-digging camps at Likatlong and Blinkkop in Griqualand West, probably because of Irma's father and her uncle Leopold's business deals in the area. They also went to see a dentist in Johannesburg. The family stayed for two weeks at the Carlton Hotel and went to see a play. Afterwards they visited the Victoria Falls in present-day Zimbabwe, with Dr Prinz accompanying them.

Although they were surrounded by Afrikaans farmers, the Sterns' cultural world was German. All the people Irma wrote about in her diary were German-speaking: Aunt Erna, Uncle Walter, Dr Prinz and her family friends Fritz, Franz Meininger and Mr Michaelis. They and their German family kept in close touch. Aunt Grete sent them special items like corsets and cream caramels from Berlin.

Like many teenagers, Irma had her good days and bad days, her emotional highs and lows. She worried particularly about personal conflicts and misunderstandings. In her diary, she noted how happy she had been to find a confidante in Aunt Erna, but how hurt and disappointed she had been to find that Aunt Erna did not keep her secrets. "When I tell her something," Irma wrote, "no matter how serious it is to me, she always teases me about it or talks about it when Doctor or Fritz are present and embarrasses me dreadfully (for I still turn red)."

Irma also recorded in her journal her mother's determination to make her pretty. "I never will be!" she lamented. Perhaps her full figure and wavy hair made it difficult for Irma to imagine herself ever being beautiful, although her mind was filled with romantic thoughts. "Love is like a fire," she wrote. "A spark leaps on to a pile of straw and immediately great flames shoot up dazzlingly."

IRMA AT THE VICTORIA FALLS, 1910

She described her crush on Fritz, whom she said was "handsome" and a "flirt", but more and more her tutor began to occupy centre stage in her emotional life. "I'm terribly fond of Dr Prinz at times," she scribbled. "He can speak in such a beautiful, gentle manner that it goes straight to one's heart."

But the Doctor could also be annoying at times:

> *Sometimes I hate him with all my heart, mainly at tennis where he doesn't behave nicely at all. I'll never show him I like him because he's sure to make fun of me. For that reason I'm often very cheeky and abrupt with him. Afterwards I'm always very sorry about it, for what can he do about it?*

Perhaps the incident that most revealed her affection for Dr Prinz is the one she describes on 10 May 1910 when the family were at home having supper. "Fritz drew our attention to the red tie Doctor was wearing," Irma wrote. "We all laughed, it looked very gaudy. Fritz pulled off the tie and it was passed from hand to hand, ending up in the Doctor's pocket."

What followed was a chase from the table to the *stoep* and then to Doctor's room, where he shut the door behind him. But that did not stop the infatuated Irma and her brother Rudi from pursuing him.

"As quickly as I could, I jumped out through the guest room window and got into Doctor's room, climbing through the window. In doing so, I pushed out a window pane and my hand was bleeding freely," she wrote. Her tutor said he could not give her the tie because it had been a present from his fiancée who had died five years before.

"Of course, this was all nonsense," Irma scoffed. "I fought for it from 8 till 11 o'clock and I finally got it too! I was tremendously excited." Later, she noted with triumph, "The tie is mine now. When I get back to Germany, I've got to give him ten red ties."

Her diary reveals that while she was in Wolmaransstad, her teenage crush on Dr Prinz and her growing awareness of her artistic talent were her main preoccupations. "I'm doing a lot of drawing at present," she noted in one entry. "For Father's birthday, I copied [a famous artist's] self-portrait. Actually, I didn't want to give away any drawing at all until I've learnt something properly, but Father would probably have been upset."

As Irma's interest in art grew, she started to read books which opened her mind to new possibilities and worlds. "When I was 15, I started to take an interest in books," Irma told a journalist from the *Cape Argus* in 1926. She had discovered and read the work of controversial writers like the Russian author Dostoevsky, "although this was taboo for me".

In the same interview, Irma revealed that her awareness of the wonder of God's creation had intensified at that time. "I now became aware that this world was quivering all over

Flower sketch done by Irma in Wolmaransstad

with splendour which could not be expressed in words and it dawned on me how wonderful it must be to grasp its magnificence and to express it through the medium of form and colour."

But how was she to achieve this task? Irma went for long walks alone, gazing at the stars and moon, so clear in this part of the country. Night after night, she sat on the windowsill pressing her nails into the wood, her heart swelling with the desire to create.

> *And then I started drawing and painting. I painted the little flowers of our dry garden, the dry grass and the distant koppies, the people around me and a dance at our house with all the quaint figures of the back veld villagers. And once I started, I never stopped again, although at that time this occupation was not allowed to be the centre of my life.*

Although she was still young, Irma had no doubt in her mind that art was her vocation. In one of her first diary entries, she noted: "Uncle Walter is always making digs. He asked me recently what I would do if I had no talent. I answered quite simply that there was no question of that, for many artists had said so already. Then he told me to my face that I was cheeky..."

Irma dreamt of growing up and studying art in Germany:

> *When I've finished school, I'll go and learn painting in Munich ... Then I'll be able to paint something properly at last! I thought Dr Prinz would be able to teach me something, but either he doesn't have much talent himself or he's put off by the fact that I have no easel. I asked Fritz to have one made for me, but I haven't seen anything yet. I'm very, very disappointed!*

The family holiday to the Victoria Falls introduced Irma to a more exotic Africa with lush vegetation, quite unlike the bleak, dry landscape around Wolmaransstad. She described "the graceful palm trees... swaying against the blue sky" and "fantastically entangled creepers" hanging down from trees, "forming garlands and swings". She recalled seeing monkeys "throwing nuts they've cracked open at one another, chattering shrilly and scampering off nimbly along the branches".

The North-West Province of her childhood had none of the lushness she had experienced in Zimbabwe. Even so, Irma still liked its barren vistas of bush, red sand and stone, heat and dust. Most wonderful of all were the sunsets, the brilliant night skies and the electrifying thunderstorms. Long afterwards when she returned to Europe, Irma remembered the amazing sense of space, heat and light in Africa.

"The sunsets are simply heavenly here," she wrote in her diary. "I'd like to transfer them to my sketch book by force. I wouldn't try painting them, for if you touch a butterfly, it loses its lustre and its gold dust."

Irma began searching for subjects to sketch and was drawn to the local Tswana people. She met a beautiful girl called Lettia who had an oval face, enigmatic smile and blinked when Irma spoke to her. Though they did not speak each other's language, Lettia agreed to sit very still and let Irma do a charcoal sketch of her.

Her diary entries also reveal Irma's love of flowers, which lasted all her life. Flowers and fruit were something she adored drawing and painting. She listed the wild flowers that grew in the Maquassi Hills around Wolmaransstad: white calla lilies, "so inviolate and charming", red pomegranate flowers, ripe, sun-warmed figs, snowy spring blossoms and prickly thorn branches.

Her year in Africa over, Irma looked forward to returning to Europe. In December 1910, the Stern family, accompanied once again by Dr Prinz, sailed to Germany via the east coast of Africa, spending New Year's in Naples, Italy.

The thought of escaping the monotony of small-town life clearly excited Irma, for she wrote in her journal, "Here one day passes like the next, like one drop of water falling after the other until the container is full and the year of my stay in Africa is over. When I get to Berlin, I'll be 16 and then life will really begin. Then I'll have dancing lessons and go to the theatre a lot. I'd love to be older!"

Little did she realise how much she would miss Africa. In an interview with the *Rand Daily Mail* in 1931, Irma confessed: "This divided upbringing was not a good one, for it [left me] with the feeling of belonging nowhere."

CHAPTER 4

Suné Raubenheimer

The Grand Ducal Saxon College of Fine Arts, Weimar

In 1911 Irma and her family returned to Berlin. It was then the third largest city in the world and was the showpiece of Kaiser Wilhelm's empire. Art, literature and drama flourished in the city.

But it was still a man's world. Women in 1911 in Germany were not allowed to vote – they were only granted this right in 1918. Not many girls had the privilege of attending university – in 1905, there were only 80 full-time female students in Germany. By 1914, this figure had grown to 4 000.

Irma was to be one of the lucky ones who got to study, but first she had to finish school. Already she was a very cultured girl. She and her mother Henny adored going to the theatre to watch operas and plays. Berlin must have been a big change from Wolmaransstad, with its bare earth and vast veld, where playing the piano or guitar was the only musical entertainment.

Both mother and daughter enjoyed all that Berlin had to offer: in winter there were balls, skating rinks and circus performances, while in summer there were open-air concerts, firework displays, balloon rides, regattas and rowing on the Spree River. At the end of May and the beginning of September, the Kaiser along with his entire court would review the army troops parading on the Tempelhof field.

Irma no longer had a tutor, but was back at school. Dr Prinz continued his studies, eventually finding a teaching position in Berlin. Irma's diary from this time is full of all the normal drama and excitement of a 16-year-old: classroom gossip, nervousness about writing exams, crushes on teachers and boys in her class and letters from an admirer, Bernard Cahn, the same boy she'd liked when she was 12. "He doesn't mean a thing to me," she wrote dismissively.

The diary records how she spent many summers with her mother's family in Einbeck, famous for its medieval buildings and local beer. Einbeck also had a sizeable Jewish community with its own synagogue.

In May 1912, Irma went to London and Paris for the first time with her mother. On their return, she did two pencil sketches of Rothenburg ob der Tauber, a Bavarian village. She loved its "enchanted Sleeping Beauty castle, a remnant of the Middle Ages".

As a teenager, Irma devoured books and read widely, from provocative German books to English works, like *Paradise and the Peri* by Thomas Moore. In her diary she discussed these books and what she thought of them. She also enjoyed attending live performances. She wrote about attending a concert in which a Mozart concerto, as well as Beethoven's Ninth Symphony, were played. She professed to be in love with a matinee idol, Alexander Moissi. "At the moment I'm pretending to be mad about Moissi," she gushed.

As she grew in maturity, Irma became increasingly aware of the importance of art. She mentioned in her journal a visit to Anna Costenoble, a painter and etcher living in Berlin. "I've been to Fräulein von Kostinobel's studio," she wrote, misspelling her name.

> *She received us in a very remarkable-looking tea gown. Then we had tea. Each cup was different from the others. Antique furniture, chandeliers, angels, carpets and a great many pictures stood and hung about. It was very pleasant ... She paints mainly*

portraits and a few still lifes (red roses) … She has also painted two allegorical pictures which I liked very much.

It is also clear from her diary that Irma, like many teenagers, had frequent clashes with her parents. For the most part, however, the 16-year-old Irma had a good relationship with her mother, who was herself only 40. But there were times when she found her mom intensely irritating. "Her bad manners at table when she lets herself go drive me quite mad," she complained.

In typical dramatic fashion, Irma related this incident when she was 18:

A few days ago, on 1 December [1912], Father ill-treated me frightfully. In my first reaction, I wanted to leave the house forever, but I couldn't because of Mother. In that case, my life … would have been very uncertain, for unfortunately I've not yet reached the stage where I can make my own living. Mother behaved with delicacy and goodness in the affair … Then I apologised to Father for the rudeness of my outburst: emotional scenes and a great reconciliation. Today it all looks like a successful tragicomedy.

While her mother treated her artistic daughter sensitively, Samuel Stern was obviously made of tougher stuff. We see this clearly in another diary entry. The family was talking about Dr Prinz, whom Irma missed terribly. "Suddenly I remembered Father's words at table which had struck me so unpleasantly. Mother asked: 'I wonder how Doctor is? It's odd that we hear nothing from him.' And Father: 'Who knows? Maybe he's shot himself.' My heart stopped at the mere thought and then I felt like crying at the coarseness of it!"

Irma's father's family background was simple and traditional. A shrewd and successful businessman, Samuel no doubt disagreed with many of his daughter's modern and romantic ideas. Referring to her father and the celebration of Rosh Hashanah, Irma wrote in September 1911:

Today is the Jewish New Year. Father is in Göttingen. I was glad. It meant I don't have to go through all the ceremonies. I'm certainly not going to fast on the Day of Atonement (Yom Kippur). I think it's quite ridiculous. It reminds me of the wild animals in the zoo who aren't fed on Wednesday and walk up and down their cages hungry. On Thursday they fling themselves on the meat as though they were crazy.

When it came to food, self-control was never one of Irma's strong points. Throughout her life, she struggled with her weight. As a teenager, she was intensely aware of how large her body was compared to others. She and her mother went on a three-week slimming course at Bad Kissingen in the summer of 1911, but it had little lasting effect. A few months later, she mentioned swimming at the baths in Berlin: "The women said my body is as mature as though I were 25. It's horrible. I'm even being robbed of my youth. What have I left?"

After their return to Germany, the Sterns had kept in touch with Dr Prinz. Irma was still very fond of him, although she had begun to despair of any real romance between them. "It seems to me as though he has been lost to me forever," she wrote in September 1911. "I don't demand any love in return. It's the first sign of growing older, this platonic, tranquil love."

A month later, however, her spirits rose when the Doctor dropped by for tea. "I'm so pleased, so happy!" she enthused. "It's wonderful to be young. I'm beautiful when I'm happy. I know that quite well. Every mirror tells me so."

Irma's sketch of Rothenburg ob der Tauber

In the midst of all the cultural activity – the visits to museums, galleries and opera houses – Irma still remembered and yearned for Africa. In her diary, she told the story of a little girl called Lisa "who lived far away in a beautiful, lonely country where there were few people, but many, many wonderful flowers", as well as monkeys, pepper trees and skulls strung up on a palm tree "so that they rattled against each other in the wind and scared off all the little birds".

It was in the middle of winter and Irma no doubt felt very homesick. Curled up with her diary, she wrote a long passage which evokes the desolate landscape of the North-West Province where she grew up: "I was in Africa one very hot day. The great gleaming sun burned down mercilessly on the long grass of the veld which had long since exchanged its fresh colour for reddish-grey. Everything seemed dry and burningly hot!"

Africa remained an important part of the Sterns' life, even when they were not living there. It was the source of Samuel's wealth and enabled the family to live a life of comfort in Germany. In March 1912, Irma noted, "Father is back in Africa again. He became too homesick. [Uncle] Leopold has bought a diamond farm, so Father had to go out."

In 1913 the Sterns made another trip back to Africa. They visited Johannesburg, Wolmaransstad and Cape Town, where Irma was thrilled to see a Malay bride and her bridesmaids driving past while she was waiting for a tram to take her to the woods in Wynberg. She went for a long walk in Bishopscourt and was very excited about her visit to the Spanish Consul, Don Luis Rubio Amoedo, who lived in Gardens. "He has the most wonderful works of art, pictures too beautiful to describe," she later wrote. His collection included paintings by the Dutch master Rembrandt van Rijn and the Baroque artist Rubens.

Their trip was a short one. After only three months in the country, the Sterns boarded the *Edinburgh Castle* in Cape Town to sail back to Europe. On board ship, Irma met the famous South African writer Olive Schreiner, author of *The Story of an African Farm*. Initially, Irma was disappointed, describing her as a "short, stout old lady". Later on, however, the two had some time together. "Olive Schreiner spoke to me a few times before the end of the voyage," she wrote. "I was delighted."

Describing their meeting in *Irma Stern, The Early Years*, Karel Schoeman wrote: "The 19-year-old Irma Stern was at the beginning of her career, while Schreiner, at 58, was nearing the end of her life – in this way, two of the most gifted women yet born in South Africa made contact with one another".

There was only one thing the young Irma ever wanted to be – an artist. And now it looked as if her dream was finally coming true. Shortly before her trip to South Africa, she had been accepted at the Grand Ducal Saxon College of Fine Arts in Weimar.

She referred once to a "fight breaking away from home" as a young adult, but in the end she managed to persuade her father that it was time for her to find her own way in life. Unlike many women of the time who never got an opportunity to study, Irma was fortunate – the art college in Weimar had a special art class for women.

She noted in her diary, "Since 4 April I've been here at the art school under Prof Frithjof Smith". This professor was a Norwegian portrait painter who had been teaching at the college for more than 20 years and was unlikely to have been up to date with the latest art trends. From the cleaner, Irma learnt that the professor "is said to be much nicer now – before his operation for gall stones, he was insufferable and also drank a lot".

A year later, in February 1914, Irma was moved to the nature class taught by Gari Melchers. He was a Dutch portrait and landscape painter who had been born in the United States and trained in the Netherlands. Irma liked him instantly. "Through the sensitive and tactful corrections he gave me, [he] appealed to me very much and helped me a good deal," she told a journalist once. Unfortunately, Melchers stayed at the academy for only another two terms, leaving Irma without a tutor.

In late 1914, a war unfolded which plunged the whole of Europe, and later the world, into conflict – World War 1. For the Stern family, there would be no more visits to South Africa for a long time. Irma found Christmas that year in Berlin very different: the joy for her had gone. "Christmas trees are fragrant in the streets," she wrote in her diary. "The rushing, warm blood is streaming – I see wasted lives, thousands, millions of men."

Irma found it difficult to celebrate "this feast of peace", while elsewhere she knew "everything is running with blood, among all these staring, dead eyes … Every festive light reminds one of the broken hearts of women, of bitter, innumerable tears shed by children, of disappointed hopes of all this horror, of the war," she wrote.

CHAPTER 5

Suné Raubenheimer

German soldiers marching off to fight in WW1

Irma continued with her studies, while World War 1 raged around her. She moved from Weimar to Berlin in search of a tutor, eventually finding Martin Brandenburg. He was a fairly modern artist who liked to paint fairytale forests and fantasies.

Irma liked his "vivid colour and fantastical subjects" and her work took a new direction. She wrote in her journal: "Under Mr Brandenburg's tuition, I now started to paint in oil, the only adequate medium for expressing one's ideas in a larger style. In him I found not only a mentor, but also a friend."

In December 1915, the Sterns spent Christmas in Einbeck, Henny's home town. A photo from this time shows her painting at an easel outdoors with a crowd of amused soldiers looking on. They had been injured on the battlefield and sent there to recover.

For three years Irma worked under Brandenburg, learning all she could. But during summer, she found it difficult to remain in the studio. "As soon as spring arrived and the days grew longer, nothing could keep me in the overheated studio," she wrote.

The kind of art Irma did at this time was still very formal and conventional. Brandenburg helped her explore Impressionist techniques, such as how to use colour and light in her paintings. In *Still Life with Green Apples*, painted in 1916, we see Irma experimenting with this style. A silver plate is made to look green because of the reflection of the tablecloth, while bright dabs of thick paint are used to suggest the shape of petals. Reflected white light is seen in the curves of the apples.

Even though Irma was growing in leaps and bounds as an artist, she still hadn't found her own style. *Das Ewige Kind* (The Eternal Child), painted in 1916, was the turning point in her development as an artist. Forty years later, Irma explained: "I painted like one painted in those days – and then, one day in a tram, opposite me, I saw a child with lanky limbs sitting, angular and awkward, with large shadowed eyes in a pale face of malnutrition. I felt compelled to draw her. I shuddered and awoke to my own generation."

She went on to say:

> *Those were the war years in Europe. I then knew what I had to express – the suffering and agony that a war means to all life. Soon after this I painted my Eternal Child – a little child with large, mistrusting eyes, with an embittered tight mouth, sitting on a chair, her plaits hanging straight off her naked forehead, her underfed hands clinging to a few field flowers … so as to assure that some beauty was always left.*

This painting ruptured her relationship with her mentor Martin Brandenburg. He found its subject matter and style deeply distasteful. Their disagreement resulted in a personal crisis for Irma. "Doubt crept into my heart," she remembered in an interview many years later. "What was art? Was my picture not the reflection of my sincerest feelings?" Eventually, she decided to leave Brandenburg's studio and forge her own path, a brave decision which proved to be the right one.

Irma continued to paint on her own, sometimes for as long as 15 hours a day. But it was only when she met the artist Max Pechstein that she really found a kindred spirit, a man whose vision and aims were very similar to hers. On seeing *The Eternal Child*, Pechstein recognised that Irma was developing as an artist and urged her to pursue this new style. Irma felt hugely encouraged. "With a few words, you cast down all the dark hours of despair and inner conflict," she told him in a letter in 1917.

Irma painting with soldiers

An Expressionist, Pechstein had an immense influence on Irma's art. Expressionism, a movement in art which lasted from 1905 to 1925, was a reaction to the formal classical style of painting so popular in Europe. Instead of trying to depict the outward reality of people, things or places, the Expressionist artist sought to express what he saw from an inner, emotional perspective.

Post-Impressionist artists like Gauguin and Van Gogh were actually forerunners of this new movement. Expressionist paintings often distorted reality for dramatic effect, making walls appear crooked or people's faces more angular and mask-like.

Expressionists felt strongly that rapid industrialisation at the start of the 20th century had had a negative effect on society. Machines and factories had had a devastating impact on life in the countryside, greatly affecting the lives of many people. Many Expressionist artists believed that by returning to the art of "primitive" people, they could help to heal their troubled society.

Expressionists loved the use of bright, violent colours which often clashed with each other. Pechstein, who was at the cutting edge of this movement, was one of the artists who founded the group known as *Die Brücke* (The Bridge) in Dresden in 1905. He and his wife Lotte travelled to the Palau islands, a Germany colony in the Pacific, in 1914.

Pechstein had found an "earthly paradise" which was to prove a rich source of inspiration for his future work. In 1920, he described his creative process, as "the crack of the brush, best of all as it stabs the canvas. Tubes of colour squeezed dry." When World War 1 began, however, he was forced to leave Palau and return to Europe to fight in the trenches.

It is not known who introduced Irma to Pechstein. All we know is that they formed a friendship in 1917. Irma later said: "To this generous and noble-minded artist, I owe more gratitude than anybody else."

For almost ten years, they wrote letters to each other, many of which Pechstein illustrated, and he visited her often to comment on her art. His first letters to her are addressed in quite a stiff, reserved way: "*Sehr geehrtes Fräulein I. Stern*", as if written to a stranger. But as their friendship grew, this soon changed to "*Liebes Fräulein I. Stern*" ("Dear Miss I. Stern"). Through Pechstein, Irma made valuable contacts which helped to establish herself more firmly as an artist.

Even so, it was not an easy time for her as a young artist. Irma painted many scenes of Africans – two young women sweeping, a portrait of a man outside a hut and a still life with palm trees. Her works from this period lack confidence, as if she was still feeling her way as an Expressionist. Perhaps because she was painting from memory, her figures lack vitality and are stick-like and spiky.

A letter from Pechstein to Irma

Still Life with Green Apples, 1916

When the paintings were exhibited for the first time in May 1919 at the Fritz Gurlitt Gallery in Berlin, they were not well received. One critic wrote, "Irma Stern paints in all kinds of modern styles. That is no disgrace, it is quite possible to begin in this way. But to put together an ambitious exhibition from such learner's attempts is something at which no one should contrive."

The fact that she was able to exhibit at all was thanks to Pechstein. He had introduced Irma to the art dealer Wolfgang Gurlitt. After meeting Gurlitt for the first time in 1918, Irma wrote in a letter to Pechstein: "He was terribly nice and my nervousness about the meeting was quite unnecessary."

In another letter, she thanked Pechstein for all his help:

> *I really can't tell you over the telephone how grateful I am to you for all the good things you have done for me! I am truly always aware of it – how wonderfully you have helped me along – how you showed me what is true and good in my work and what is empty phrasing, and then how you have helped me with other people and have smoothed the path for me.*

Irma felt honoured when in November 1918, she was invited to become a member of the *Novembergruppe* (the November group), an artists' collective run by Pechstein and others. Its aim was to achieve a revolution in the arts, similar to the social upheaval that Germany was experiencing in the aftermath of World War 1, a war which claimed 18 million lives.

Irma commented about this invitation in an interview: "I considered this a very flattering offer, since besides a sculptress, I was the only woman who had been asked to join this society."

Living in Germany during the war meant having to face food shortages. Many people had to replace potatoes with turnips as a staple food, while roasted soy flour and saccharine had to take the place of coffee and sugar. (This kind of food was called *ersatz* in German, meaning an inferior substitute.)

But it seems that the Sterns were better off than many others. On at least two occasions, Irma was able to send her friend Pechstein food parcels.

The war took an emotional toll on Irma and it seems from her letters that she was homesick. Writing to Pechstein in May 1918, Irma said:

> *The sun no longer pours out her full love and warmth over us in this fourth autumn of the war. I suddenly feel uprooted – I stare after the migrating birds with intense longing and can find no rest and tranquillity for work. Berlin makes me so tired – there's no real spring here.*

We know that in June 1920 she and her family were preparing to leave Germany, because she wrote to another friend:

> *I must write to you, although I tell myself a thousand times so many moons and people lie between us, and yet the thought of leaving Europe drives me to it. My days pass in senseless preparation, everything monotonous, sober and lacking in harmony.*

The Sterns had been living in Berlin for seven years – the longest period Irma had spent in one place up to this point. Now they were packing up again to go to Africa, the warm, vibrant Africa of her childhood. It was a thought that filled Irma with boundless excitement. Having received an excellent artistic training, she was now ready to paint real African subjects.

CHAPTER 6

Suné Raubenheimer

FLOWER SELLERS IN ADDERLEY STREET, 1921

Irma described her first glimpse of Cape Town on the deck of a ship as follows:

Daybreak; the steamer's engine slows down. Soon we will be there. Africa – the word was the personification of everything desirable to me. The land of my childhood. The sun – its brown people – its sheer mountains. The endless sky. The splendour of its flowers saturated with colour. The fruit with its sweet and yet so sharp fragrance.

There it lay before me now, lights glittering in the dimness before the day. Jagged dark mountains – the most delicate heaven above. How would it be, this Africa, after all the years of yearning and waiting?

Poor Irma – ever the idealist – was bitterly disappointed when she set foot in the Mother City in 1920. She found the English hotel where her family stayed dreary and boring – "like mineral water gone flat".

On a whim, she decided to climb Table Mountain. A rustling in the yellow grass alerted her to a tortoise. She picked it up and it peed on her in fright. Irma laughed in delight.

"This was the first scrap of nature – the first scrap of originality… It was still the same Africa as years ago and the earth still smelled of the heat of the sun in the same pungent way," she wrote years later of the experience.

Irma's journal sketch of fleeing Europe after WW1

It must have been quite a culture shock for the 26-year-old Irma, settling into Cape Town, with a tiny population of 188 000 people, compared to the size and sophistication of Berlin. She probably found it uncomfortable to be speaking English instead of German.

Cape Town at that time was a small, compact city. The city centre featured old Victorian, Edwardian and Cape Dutch buildings and the sea still covered large parts of what we now call the Foreshore. The Malay and Coloured population had not yet been pushed out to the fringes of the city – this was only to happen later in the 1950s and 1960s under apartheid – and they shared in the daily life and bustle of the city.

Culturally, Cape Town seemed more like Europe than Africa. This must have been a disappointment at first for Irma. "One leads a civilised life, almost like Germany," she wrote to her friend Trude Bosse a year after arriving in the Mother City. "The people are only interested in making money."

In the spring of 1921, the Sterns moved into a rented house, 34 Breda Street in Oranjezicht on the slopes of Table Mountain. They lived there until early 1925.

Irma had a bedroom decorated with carved wooden furniture and her own art collection. She fell in love with the plants in the garden – golden shower creepers, palm trees, vines and fig trees. It was at Coblentz Villa that she painted a tree bursting forth with poinsettias, with Lion's Head in the background. In another letter to Trude, Irma wrote, "The world is so beautiful here, so indescribably beautiful."

By 1922, Irma felt she was ready to exhibit some of her artwork. She held an exhibition in February at Ashbey's Gallery in Long Street. It consisted of 96 watercolours, oil paintings, hand-printed woodcuts, lithographs and drawings. Most of the oil paintings were on sale for £20 or £30, a fraction of their worth today.

Lion's Head and Poinsettias, 1921

Judging by the titles of the paintings, they portrayed typical South African scenes: *Hermanus*, *Malay Couple*, *Coloured Girl with Sunflowers*, *On the Zambezi*, *Native Girl*, *Native Dance*, *Zulu Woman* and *Nurse Maid with Baby*. Strangely enough, the exhibition also featured some fabric Irma had painted, including table cloths, girls' dresses and even a tea cosy!

The man who opened the exhibition was Dominee GFC Faustman of

Wynberg, formerly of Schweizer-Reneke, who was an old family friend. Irma's parents no doubt thought it was important for someone of standing to launch their daughter's first South African art exhibition.

Perhaps it was a good idea, for Irma's style was completely different from what most art lovers in Cape Town were used to. They had never encountered Expressionism before and were used to the style of Romantic Realism that was popular at the time. They probably found her use of bold colour and the strangely twisted figures rather disturbing.

ANOTHER SKETCH OF ARRIVING IN "THE LAND OF STRONG COLOURS"

The *dominee* was tactful: "I am not qualified to judge her art," he said, "although those in the know say it's very good... Above all, Miss Stern is original. She has her own way of looking at things."

But others were not so kind. "The people who attended... were completely mystified," wrote one Cape Town art collector. An Afrikaans critic in *Die Burger* said Irma's paintings lacked harmony and balance. But *The Cape Times* art reviewer had the cruellest things to say. He expressed his "disgust at the general nastiness of the work" and declared that "no serious attention need to be paid to this attempt to startle... Cape Town art lovers".

The 27-year-old Irma must have found been crushed by these reviews, especially since her paintings had been well received in Berlin. There was one consolation: her art had caused a mild sensation in Cape Town and attracted large crowds of people. The *Cape Argus* wrote on 11 February:

> *As a draw to the public, no show of pictures has ever succeeded like the exhibition by Miss Stern now on view at Ashbey's Galleries. There is a constant stream of visitors throughout the day and once at least during the lunch hour, the crowd was so great that waiting queues had to be formed.*

The pettiness of colonial life in Cape Town annoyed Irma intensely. To her German friend Trude, she wrote: "Everything that's new – and almost everything is new to these narrow-minded people – is simply laughed at, scorned and afterwards, imitated. It's so unpleasant living in the restrictions of such a small town."

***Umgababa*, 1922**

For the free-spirited Irma, living in such close quarters with her parents was also a challenge. She found life with her domineering mother and father stifling.

"It's as though the life with my parents robs me of all strength to live myself, it's like a constant pressure," she complained to Trude. For someone who had once wanted to be a dancer, Irma was upset that her parents would not even let her do ballroom dancing. She felt "controlled" and "turned into a child – in spite of all the pampering and luxury".

Irma longed to get away and experience Africa in a raw, unspoilt way – and her opportunity came later that same year. "I went on my way until one day, like a sign from heaven, a vision led me to the place where I believed myself able to hear the heartbeat of Africa – Umgababa," she wrote.

Umgababa is a tiny village on the KwaZulu-Natal South Coast. Staying at the Beach Hotel, Irma was delighted with the tropical vegetation, the bright hibiscus flowers and the lush pawpaws, bananas and other fruit – and gave herself over completely to her art.

At the hotel Irma met Nancy Gele, a young Zulu laundrywoman. They became friends and Nancy promised to show her the Umgababa beyond the tourist experience. She invited Irma to the homestead of a family of potters.

Irma was enthralled by the demonstration given by the Zulu potter and his wife who made "beautiful, gleaming black vessels … with sparing ornamentation," as well as the Zulu dancing at a wedding feast.

Umgababa - South Coast
Beach Hotel
Anfang Sept. 1922
Liebe Trude – wie klingt Dir das – Umgababa –? Es ist gerade so – wie ich mir das Paradies vorstelle. Wir wohnen dicht am Meere – einem wild tobenden Meere – Palmen rings um uns herum – Bananenpalmen. –
So ungefähr liegt das Haus.

Irma's letter to Trude, Umgababa, 1922

Writing later in her travel journal, she recounted her experiences there: "The men formed a double circle – the wiry bodies tense, listening. The dance leader waved a staff to which an animal skin was fastened. The dance began. Slow, measured movement, inflexible rhythm, panting power, wild cries, flying limbs, movement set free."

This rhythm and movement is seen in the paintings Irma did during this time. In *Umgababa*, we see the portrayal of an ideal, timeless Africa, broken by the railway line which cuts through the middle of the painting like a scar. There is a tension between the traditional African way of life and the modernisation brought about by the West. Stormy rain clouds brood in the sky.

Since leaving Germany, Irma had been searching for the real Africa: an Africa where black people were free and lived their life in harmony with nature, untouched by the modern world. Now, in Umgababa, she had finally found it and it was a life-changing discovery. As an Expressionist, she felt she had arrived at the source, the very beginning of all things – the Garden of Eden. This was an Africa unlike the dusty, dry veld of her childhood, an Africa she had only had inklings of before.

The time Irma spent in Umgababa was of huge importance in her growth as an artist. Not only was she free to paint the Africa of her dreams, but she was developing greater mastery of her medium. Writing to Trude, she said: "The pictures fell into my lap like ripe pears falling on the grass in autumn… It's as though waves laden with fertility were breaking over my head."

DAS PARADIS, IRMA'S DESCRIPTION OF FINDING THE SOURCE OF CREATIVITY

Umgababa was a confirmation to Irma that the Africa she had always longed for actually existed. Unlike the wooden and one-dimensional paintings of African women sweeping or gathering berries she had done in Germany, she was now capturing real, complex subjects. She had found her true calling. On a scrap of paper in Umgababa dated 3 September 1922, Irma scribbled: "The artist creates in order to become free of himself, only to find himself again in the end."

CHAPTER 7

Suné Raubenheimer

Irma's house, The Firs

In May 1923, having spent almost three years in South Africa, Irma was again filled with wanderlust and was delighted when her parents offered to take her with them to Europe. On the trip to Germany on board the ship, the *Usaramo*, Irma met and fell madly in love with Hippolyto Raposo, a Portuguese writer and professor who had taken part in the Portuguese Revolution of 1910.

"He told me of his life, of his books, which he himself had written, of the revolution in his country and how he … had been imprisoned," recalled Irma. Unfortunately for the 29-year-old Irma, Hippolyto, then 37, was already engaged to someone else, so she knew from the start that there was no future for them together.

Two years later in Johannesburg, Irma poured out her heart as she recalled the memorable sea voyage in which she had found and lost the "eternal friend" she had been searching for since childhood:

He could not speak my language, nor I his, and yet no one has ever understood my words so well, never. And I knew immediately that he was bound to a foreign woman, bound by the words of convention, and I knew too that I could be with him for 12 days only – 12 days and then he would join his fiancée – 12 days. A sword was lodged in my heart – slowly, quietly, it bled, from the first moment. And I could not show him how I suffered…

It would be easy to scoff at the intensity of Irma's feelings for this man she barely knew, but it's important to remember that Irma had an artistic temperament. This meant that she felt the highs and lows of life more intensely than others. In some ways, this was a gift – her intensity enabled her to create beautiful paintings using vibrant colours – but in her personal relationships, it often felt like a curse.

This is certainly true when it came to her love life. She cried many tears over her failed romance with Hippolyto and kept the signed book he gave her for the rest of her life. It bears this inscription: "To Irma Stern, presented in admiration of your art, with the wish that you may learn to love the soul of Portugal..."

Arriving in Europe, Irma and her parents were greeted with upheaval. Germany was in the grip of strikes and riots, soaring prices and political instability. The Nazi Party, which was established in 1920, was fast gaining support. While the Sterns were visiting in 1923, the Nazis tried to seize power in Munich, resulting in Adolf Hitler's arrest and imprisonment.

Despite these troubled times, Irma managed to have successful exhibitions in Berlin, elsewhere in Germany and in Vienna. In September 1923, the reviewer in *Das Kunstblatt* wrote: "Although African by birth and still at home in the bush, she paints exotic humanity and landscapes in the European manner, seen through Pechstein's eyes, as it were."

The Sterns visited London, Paris and Italy before returning to Cape Town in January 1924. Irma threw herself back into her art and also into the social life of the city. She helped arrange the Three Arts Ball that year. A magazine article describes her being carried into the City Hall on the night of the ball, dressed as a Persian princess on a "gorgeous, silk-draped, canopied litter, painted in rich designs of red and gold and flaming crimson." Her elaborate costume, complete with peacock feathers, jewels, embroidery and pink chiffon trousers, won her a prize.

Irma was also a member of the K Club, which was formed in 1922 to "bring together those interested in the arts and crafts of the present day." The well-known painter Ruth Prowse played a leading role in this club.

How did those who knew her well see her? Two of her Jewish friends, Roza van Gelderen and Hilda Purwitsky, described Irma as both outgoing and shy in an article they wrote for the *South African Jewish Chronicle*:

> *[She is] … vivacious, bright and sunny, with a silvery, gurgling laugh. She is very impulsive, taking quick likes and dislikes to people. Her judgements are often based on intuition rather than on reason, but they are seldom at fault. Slightly temperamental, she is subject to momentary depressions, which are, however, easily dispelled. She is a little shy of strangers and only her keen interest in the possibilities in people makes her willing to meet them. With her friends, she is merry and a sympathetic companion.*

Her German childhood friend, Trude Bosse, who exchanged dozens of letters with Irma throughout her life, recalls a different Irma:

> *She really led a most restless life. She was disappointed and depressed most of the time and felt that life gave her more suffering than she could bear … I doubt if she was ever happy – perhaps only for a little while. She was restless and pleasure-seeking, loved eating and drinking and even smoked the occasional cigar.*

It would seem that Irma was very unhappy about her appearance. The pretty little girl was now a rather large woman with frizzy hair. She had the force of personality and a keen mind to make up for her rather unattractive appearance. But probably to console herself, Irma bought things that fitted her easily – hats and shoes.

Regardless of how she may have felt about herself, Irma clearly possessed some powers of attraction. Johannes Prinz, the man who had been her tutor when she was growing up in Schweizer-Reneke, became a suitor in 1921. He had arrived in South Africa that year to further his studies.

In the beginning, Irma rebuffed Prinz's advances, finding him a bore.

She was in love with somebody else at the time, but her parents did not approve of him. Writing to Trude, she said:

> *Dr Prinz, whom you already know, came out and wanted to marry me and there I sit – the one I can't have, the other I don't want … At home there is discord as a result and I feel extremely unhappy. For the man with whom I would like to be isn't here – the other one is around me from morning till night.*

Prinz made a favourable impression on Irma's parents. He had become a lecturer in the German department at the University of Cape Town and he wrote a number of newspaper and magazine articles on modern art. By December 1922, he was living with the Sterns. He was still trying to woo Irma, but to little avail. "Prinz is still in the house," Irma complained in a letter to Trude. "Friendship has been built up artificially between us. He is full of what's past; with me everything is dead."

In 1924, after Irma had returned from Europe, she and Prinz attended the Jazz Masque Ball together. They dressed up as an Egyptian pharaoh and his wife.

At around this time, Irma visited Swaziland, which was to make a lasting impression on her. She found the Swazi women incredibly beautiful and enjoyed painting them. In a German magazine, *Frau und Gegenwart*, she wrote about her experience:

> *Today I accepted an invitation to Swaziland. The car drove through lonely regions to an isolated village consisting of only a few huts. And here in front of a hut I found three girls of magical, colourful loveliness which I immediately tried to capture... They stood pressed close together. All three of them had their hair cut in the same way and coloured with white chalk. Colourful cloths were wrapped around their bodies, their slender wrists and ankles encircled with a thread of coloured wool, the same colour which I found at the throat. They were dainty and graceful and I thought that I had never seen so much beauty together. They conducted me to their queen and advised me to take along her favourite delicacy as a present: caterpillars – beautiful, fat, live caterpillars.*

THREE SWAZI SISTERS, 1925

This encounter was rendered into the painting *Three Swazi Sisters*, which Irma noted in her clippings book as having been painted in 1925 and sold in Paris for £35.

Later that year, while on holiday on KwaZulu-Natal's South Coast, Irma received a letter from Prinz. It was a light-hearted, teasing letter, addressing her as *Liebes Sternchen* (Darling Little Miss Stern) and signed with the nickname "Dok" (short for Doctor, a reference to when he was her tutor). This was the first sign that their relationship was progressing into a romance.

A few months later, on 1 April 1926, the couple was married by special licence. The fact that Prinz had recently been promoted to professor at UCT may have strengthened Irma's parents' belief that he was a suitable match for her. The witnesses to the wedding were her father, Samuel Stern, and a family friend, Miriam Levy. Irma was 31 years old and Prinz 40. Irma's mentor, Max Pechstein, sent a letter of congratulations with a sketch of himself strewing roses over the path of the married couple strolling towards a busy harbour.

Two picture studies by Irma, 1926

The newly-weds moved into a rented house in Sea Point. A year later, after another long visit to Europe, Irma bought, in her own name, The Firs in Chapel Road, Rosebank. It was a gracious double-storied Victorian home with an imposing front entrance and a driveway which wound through the large garden. Nestled on the lower slopes of Devil's Peak, it was very close to the university and had a sweeping view of the Cape Flats and the Hottentots Holland Mountains in the distance.

Irma loved to travel, but this was her home until the day she died. Wherever she was in the world, she always had The Firs to come back to. It was her sanctuary, the place where she could paint in peace in her studio, where she could entertain her friends with sumptuous meals and show off her extensive antique collection.

She hired Charlie, a butler from Zanzibar, and a local cook who helped her prepare meals to impress, sometimes insisting that each course contained food of the same colour. After her death, thanks to the efforts of her friend Freda Feldman, The Firs became the Irma Stern Museum.

Irma put her own stamp on the house. A 1929 article in the South African Jewish magazine *Ivri Onouchi* described her studio as "a most enchanting room, with three walls of a pale yellow colour and the fourth a bright and happy orange". The article went on to describe the studio in more detail:

> *All about the wall hung canvases pinned onto wooden frames. Some stood on easels or lay rolled up on the floor in piles. A huge flamboyant palette shared a table with dozens of brushes, cigarette tins, ash trays, sketches, packets of seed (for she is a great gardener) and a little vase containing a precious flower. French windows open onto a lovely garden riotous with colour like the pictures its flowers inspire.*

Irma adored flowers and pottered around happily in the huge garden at The Firs. She proudly wrote to Trude about the "larkspur, stocks, enormous geraniums, all shades of pelargoniums, great balls of white and also yellow daisies, violet and yellow poppies, sunflowers and many, many roses, carnations, petunias, fuchsias."

In another letter, she described the intense colours in her garden:

> *Our roses are all snow-white, the earth yellow-red – a giant dark cypress stands in the garden – flaming red geraniums against the white walls in jade green jars, the oak trees are yellow-brown, the mountain like a soul, constantly changing – it's all beautiful.*

Unfortunately Irma's marriage to Prinz was not a fulfilling one. Perhaps her parents, who were still supporting Irma financially, had placed too much pressure on her. They thought Prinz would be the ideal husband – he was German, well bred and financially secure. (Irma's other love interests had either lacked social status or been short of money or both.)

It seems that even though Prinz was intellectually her equal, he was not able to relate to his wife emotionally. Sadly, the loneliness that Irma had felt as a single woman continued after she was married.

In the beginning, Irma seemed happy enough. Her husband, after all, was an academic and spent a lot of his time on research, which may explain why they didn't connect much. Irma painted two portraits of Prinz in which he appears larger and more masculine than he was in real life.

"My husband Jan and I get on well together – that's the main thing," Irma wrote to Trude a few months after their marriage. They were certainly fond of each other, for in a letter that Prinz wrote to Irma in September 1931, while she was staying in Madeira, Portugal, he told her that the roses and carnations in their garden at home were flourishing and sent her birthday greetings, as well as some gifts: a two-year subscription to an art magazine, a book on the artist Hieronymus Bosch and "a beautiful dress" which she could buy on his account.

It seems he missed his wife so much that he wrote, "This loneliness is quite dreadful. I am glad that a large part of this trial is already over."

Most of the letters he wrote to Irma date from the visit he made to Germany between December 1932 to June 1933, hoping to obtain treatment for his encephalitis, a disease affecting the brain. His long typed letters to Irma reflect his despondency about finding a cure for his condition. But he always asked Irma questions about her art and their domestic life, showing his concern for her.

Even though she was now married, Irma continued to live the restless gypsy life to which she had grown accustomed as a child. She was often away from home for long periods. In March 1926, she went on a tour of the interior of South Africa. In a newspaper interview, she spoke of her trip, saying, "I travelled through a part of the country where all motorists said: 'You will never get through, the road is impassable, the scenery very fine, but we warn you'."

In another article in 1929, her friend Hilda Purwitsky wrote of her "lengthy" expeditions into Mozambique, the Transkei, Swaziland and Zululand:

> *Usually, she makes for a little trading station in the heart of a big area uninhabited by white men. Only one white trader is to be found for miles and miles around and there she takes up her abode. Africans come in from outlying districts to buy and to barter. They come in little parties and when they are at the station, she gets them in groups, making no effort to pose them. There is something friendly, tolerant and pleasant about Irma Stern that makes one soon feel at ease with her and it is evident from her work that her subjects must feel that, too...*

Their thoughts seem miles away. Some stand, others sit. They chat to one another; they are probably discussing her in their musical language.

Once she started travelling and discovering the rural villages and interesting characters that lived in them, Irma was hooked. It was the fuel that she needed to drive her art forward.

In 1927, she went on another visit to Swaziland, this time for eight weeks, staying for a while at Ezulwini, a trading station near the capital, Mbabane. "There she was called upon by King Sobhuza, who invited her to be present at a dance at the royal kraal," the *Cape Argus* reported.

Two years later, Irma took a trip to Pondoland in the Eastern Cape. Driving from Port St John's, she came across a beautiful valley called Mgweyana, which she related in an interview with the *SA Jewish Chronicle*:

To her intense delight, she did find one house and a shop there. It was owned by a Jew. This Jewish storekeeper and his daughters, on being asked for accommodation, had a little discussion, then diffidently offered her the best they could – two rondavels ... Here she worked for some weeks and found rich material in the Mpondo people who came every day to the Jew's store.

Swaziland in particular impressed her. "Irma Stern was enchanted by the Swazis whom, she says, are a very musical people," a 1929 article in *Ivri Onouchi* observed.

As an Expressionist, the call of the "exotic" was very strong in her: she felt drawn to depict people in their traditional surroundings. Having close and intense encounters with people from different cultures was a tonic for her. From 1922 to 1929, Irma's confidence and style as an artist grew rapidly.

Pondo Woman, 1924

Irma's sketch of her husband, Johannes Prinz, shortly after they married

And as she painted, her body of work continued to expand. By 1925, she was ready for her second exhibition, again held at Ashbey's in Cape Town. A total of 96 paintings were displayed, with titles such as *Zulu Woman*, *Zulu Girl* and *Witch Doctor*. She also exhibited a sequence depicting a Chinese theatrical troupe she had met on a trip to Johannesburg. The following year she exhibited in Cape Town, Bloemfontein and Johannesburg. Her fourth exhibition at Ashbey's in February 1929 included many Swazi paintings, such as *Swazi Woman amidst Bamboo* and *Hairdressing*, as well as other portraits, landscapes and still lifes.

Unfortunately for Irma, it was some time before the South African art-loving public began to appreciate her unique style. The 1925 exhibition was greeted with "storms of abuse and denunciation", according to Hilda Purwitsky. She wrote in her review:

> *When her second exhibition was opened a few weeks ago in Cape Town, the crowds were no less numerous. It was rather amusing to observe that the most varying types of spectators attend her*

show, among them people who never think of coming to an art gallery in the ordinary way.

What struck Hilda most forcibly in the exhibition was Irma's strong use of colour.

Colours, wild, shrieking, crude, fling themselves at the onlooker. Rank, luxuriant vegetation and massive tropical blooms display such marvellous virility … And again one is dragged back to the colours. There is something crazy in that abundance of colour – harsh and blinding and immoderate … There is no apparent law and order there – only a reckless, smothering turmoil.

It is true to say that Irma's art was met with bewilderment. A reviewer in Bloemfontein wrote, "Though we may not like or understand the work shown, it remains of interest as an example of a new type of art."

Irma as a young artist in her studio

Some reviewers were not so kind. "Freak Picture Exhibition" ran the headlines of a Johannesburg newspaper, along with "Art of Miss Irma Stern: Ugliness as a Cult."

This second article was probably written by the critic Hedley A. Chilvers, who elsewhere had admitted that he found Irma's work interesting: "It repels and yet it attracts. It is mysterious." Only one reviewer in the *Cape Times* put her work in context, saying, "Once we have ignored the six thousand miles that isolate us from Europe and realised that art is constantly progressing, then we are in a position to appreciate the work of Miss Stern."

Ironically, Europe at the time had already moved beyond Expressionism. By the early 1920s, a new movement had begun to replace it – Realism or *Neue Sachlichkeit* (new objectivity), as it was known in Germany.

By 1921, the poet Ivan Goll lamented that "Expressionism is at its last gasp". Its death knell was probably in 1925, when the *Neue Sachlichkeit* exhibition opened in Mannheim, marking the end of Expressionism's popularity.

But because Irma lived so far away in South Africa, she was unaffected by the changing tides in European art. Ignoring the latest fads as well as her critics, she continued to develop her craft in the style she had made her own.

Irma in her garden at The Firs

Das Ewige Kind (The Eternal Child), 1916

***Swazi Youth*, 1929**

Transvaal Landscape, 1933

***Flowers and Fruit*, 1937**

Watussi Queen, 1943

Arab Youth, 1945

MALAY WEDDING, 1957

Pimento Harvest, 1962

CHAPTER 8

Suné Raubenheimer

Nazi soldiers warn Germans not to buy from Jewish shops in 1933

Irma accompanied her parents to Germany at the end of 1926.

Looking forward to the trip, Irma wrote to her friend Trude Bosse: "I long for people with intellect again."

By now her work was widely appreciated in Germany and she revelled in the attention she received. She was featured in newspaper articles and in a review of her exhibition at the Gurlitt Gallery, alongside another well-known Expressionist, Karl Schmidt-Rottluff.

There is no doubt that Berlin at that time was very alive artistically. Despite political and economic turbulence during the period between the two World Wars, there was an upsurge of activity in the arts, literature and music, particularly in Berlin.

"Everything was quite immediate in Berlin," said the writer Elias Canetti. "Every kind of influence was permissible; no one was denied the right to draw attention to himself as long as he didn't mind making the effort."

Another German writer, Carl Zuckmayer, was rather blunt about Berlin: "The city devoured talents and human energies with a ravenous appetite, grinding them small, digesting them or rapidly spitting them out again."

Even though by this time Irma had spent much of her life in South Africa, she still considered herself German, both in terms of language and culture. The frequent trips she made in the 1920s to Germany bear testimony to the close bond she had with this country, which – though she did not realise it then – was about to be ripped apart.

Fisherman, Madeira, 1931

It was not only in Germany that Irma's art was recognised. On a second trip to Europe with her family in 1927, she won a prize at the International Exhibition of Fine Art in Bordeaux, France. Later that year she had an exhibition in Paris, followed by others in Brussels, Vienna, Amsterdam and the Hague.

Unfortunately for her, the exhilarating highs of her acclaim in Europe were in sharp contrast with the lows when she returned to South Africa. "After the tempo of Europe, suddenly nothing, yawning emptiness," she wrote to her friend Trude.

Irma could not understand how she could be brimming over with ideas and longing to get back to work in her Cape Town studio and then feel completely stifled when she eventually returned. "Do you know when one enters a vacuum, one dies from lack of air, even though one's lungs were full. I've got a head full of things to do – full of joy in creating – suddenly it's all empty."

Her third trip to Europe in 1929 included Germany, the Netherlands and Belgium. Her husband came with too – he wanted to do some historical research for a book he was writing. Their final visit before the Nazis came to power was from 1931 to 1932. Irma's parents went to Bad Kissingen, the same spa town the family had visited when Irma was a little girl, but Irma chose to stay behind by herself on the Portuguese island of Madeira. Perhaps she went in search of "the soul of Portugal", as the writer Hippolyto had urged her to do many years before.

Irma was only too happy to be left alone to paint – she worked hard, completing many pictures and was fascinated by life in Madeira, its people and their traditions, even though she could not speak a word of Portuguese.

This was the first time that Irma had found inspiration outside of Africa. Perhaps she felt she'd exhausted all the artistic possibilities in Zululand, Swaziland and Pondoland. Perhaps she wanted a change in scenery.

When she was hanging her paintings for an exhibition in Paris, it dawned on her that she was using a very small range of colours in her art work. The art reviewer in *The Star* in June 1931 expressed her realisation in this way:

> *The brown... of her subjects, with orange, red and green, were domineering colours in her canvases and this made her think that her palette was limited, except for a few still lifes in which*

she saw a wealth of colour schemes and on those still lifes she determined to build up her work.

Irma loved being in Madeira – it had an invigorating effect on her. "Madeira, to me a wordless concept of earliest delights," she wrote. "Sun and bright colours and beautiful children with big, dark eyes. Flowers covering the walls of the brightly coloured houses." What she saw reminded her of her childhood memories, "and yet they are somehow so firmly anchored in the blood that the words one day ripened like a slow, creeping fever. I had to go to Madeira."

In a letter she wrote to her friend Roza van Gelderen, Irma said, "You cannot imagine how interesting this all is for me. But how I ever can go away from here and feel happy again, I do not know – it is so full of beauty and colour and life."

But there were things that upset her on the island. One was the English hotel in which she stayed – "everything somehow like something from a world in which one no longer feels at home, the people, the things, old, musty," she said. Another was the way men seemed to treat women. She wrote, "Only the women look depressed, the women are like the cows – they work in the fields – in the houses – they drag heavy loads – they bring a number of children into the world and look upon it without joy themselves – grown sour somehow with deep lines around the mouths."

Irma stayed on the eastern coast of Madeira in a town called Santa Cruz. Although it was the perfect holiday spot, she worked exceptionally hard. "I'm living in a delightful fisherman's village," she told Roza. "But I am a bit overworked, as I have not much otherwise to distract me. I go on working all day."

Later, in an interview published in the *Cape Times*, she said she could have stayed a year there if she had been able to keep up the intensive pace of work: "But feeling she needed a rest, she went over to London and while there gave a very successful exhibition of some of her Madeira work."

Some believe that Irma had a nervous breakdown while she was on the island. This may have been for personal reasons – she was working too hard and her marriage was falling apart. But she was also influenced by the mood in Europe at the time. A dangerous undercurrent of hatred towards Jews was gathering force in Germany.

Irma probably understood the reasons for this hostility. Many Germans were poor because of the high rate of unemployment and they resented the way their country had been treated after World War 1. They saw how some Jewish people lived and the businesses they owned – and this made Germans bitter.

Tapping into this bitterness, the Nazi Party rose in popularity, especially as the full brunt of the Great Depression began to be felt. So cleverly did the Nazis exploit the fears and anger of ordinary Germans that when a Nazi speaker compared the Jews to bugs in a speech he gave in 1932 and demanded that they be eliminated, he was greeted with hearty applause.

"The cry *Juda, Verrecke* (Jews, drop dead) became commonplace," wrote the historian George Mosse. Even more chilling, he said, was the song sung by Nazi Storm Troopers as they marched through the streets: "When Jewish blood drips from the knife..."

When she returned to South Africa in 1932, Irma began to exhibit her work. This time, instead of being met with ridicule and rejection, more and more people appreciated her art. Perhaps this was because another South African artist, Maggie Laubser, who had visited Europe in the 1920s and been influenced by the Expressionists, had started to experiment with this style.

Gradually the art critics in South Africa began to understand Expressionism. In 1932 Irma held an exhibition in Cape Town, followed by others in Pretoria and Johannesburg.

How the tide had turned! Her first exhibition in the country had been roundly rejected. People thought her work was worthless. Now Irma Stern was being celebrated as "the greatest creative artist in South Africa today," according to the *Cape Times*.

She was the only South African artist who was asked to contribute works at the annual exhibition at the Imperial Gallery of Art in London in 1929. That same year, the mining magnate Ernest Oppenheimer bought one of her works for the South African National Gallery.

In 1932 a painting of Irma's was purchased for the new South African embassy in London, and two of her paintings were acquired for the Pretoria City Hall the following year. It had taken ten years of hard work, but finally Irma had won the art community over. It must have been a very satisfying moment.

But although her career was flourishing, strains were appearing in Irma's marriage because of her husband's ill health. In May 1933, Prinz spent many months in Germany for medical treatment, leaving Irma alone. She decided to fill her time by taking a long trip into the remote interior.

The trip was not only very long – 11 000km in total – but also disappointing. Irma was dismayed at how much traditional life had changed, especially in Swaziland, a country she was very fond of.

"It was a shock to me to see how the natural picturesqueness of the African in his kraal had almost entirely disappeared," she said in an interview printed in the *Cape Argus* in July 1933:

> *Six years ago I saw him as a joyous, untrammelled creature, the spirit of Africa at its happiest and most colourful. Today he has submitted to civilisation. He wears everyday clothes and boots. He looks odd and drab in his garb and its unnaturalness seems to have cramped his spirit. The joy of life is no longer there. He seems unhappy in the burden of civilised living. To those of us who saw beauty in the African in his natural state, the change is sad.*

In order to rediscover the exotic, Irma would have to travel further afield: to Zanzibar and the Congo or on more trips to Madeira. But she did not give up on her own country entirely.

Springtime in Namaqualand, 1933

In September 1933 she took another car trip with her mother to Namaqualand in the Northern Cape, famous for its wild flowers in spring. As a result, the exhibition Irma gave in February 1934 featured far more landscapes and still lifes than portraits of Africans.

Irma's ties to South Africa were strengthening, while her attachment to Germany was weakening. In January 1933 the Nazi Party finally came to power. It was the end of an era for Irma: the artists' cafés near her old house in Berlin were half-empty. Those Jews and intellectuals who still gathered around the marble tables "spoke in low, scared voices", afraid of being arrested, according to the writer Christopher Isherwood.

The Nazis immediately began to persecute Jewish people in Germany, boycotting their businesses. In April 1933, posters were placed in shop windows owned by Jews which said, "Germans! Defend yourselves! Do not buy from Jews."

This alarmed Irma. "I get terribly frightened when I think of Germany's future," she wrote to Trude Bosse. "So much hatred that has to be overcome and so much blood that has to be shed."

Irma's husband Johannes Prinz, who was in Germany when Hitler became Chancellor, did not seem at all bothered by events there, such as the burning of "un-German" books. Writing to Irma, he said, "I have read a great deal lately, but very little that was worthwhile. Let's hope that contemporary literature may also experience a resurgence under Hitler's guiding hand!" Speaking to the *Cape Times* a few months later, he said "the accounts we hear of Germany are vastly exaggerated."

But for Irma, what was happening in Germany was deeply shocking. She had never been a very devout Jew, but neither had she ever made any attempt to hide the fact that she was Jewish. Most of her friends were Jewish, her family was Jewish and she featured regularly in Jewish publications in South Africa.

Perhaps what affected her most was the treatment of her former mentor, Max Pechstein, also a Jew. He was branded an "unacceptable" artist and expelled from the Berlin Academy, where he was a professor. His work was removed from public art galleries because the Nazis deemed it "degenerate" – altogether, around 326 of his paintings disappeared from public view.

Thankfully, Irma's immediate family was safe, having left Germany years before. However, two of her aunts died during World War 2: one of them at her home at the age of 83, the other in a concentration camp at Theresienstadt.

The fact that her husband did not seem to mind that the Nazis had seized power in Germany is perhaps just one more reason why Irma and Prinz grew apart. The other is that his health was worsening. Perhaps she had never really loved him, but had been persuaded into the marriage by her parents.

Johannesburg exhibition, 1936

After returning from her road trip to Namaqualand in October 1933, she wrote a formal note to him in English: "I have come to the conclusion that our marriage is a failure and I have decided to leave you." The divorce was granted in March 1934.

Besides never having been passionately in love with Prinz, Irma probably found it hard to juggle her responsibilities as a wife and an artist. For her, art came first and her marriage was a very distant second. Forced to choose between her career, which was beginning to flourish, and a marriage that was drained of affection, she chose her art, which had always been her first love.

After the divorce, Prinz remained on the staff at the University of Cape Town, but he was often absent for medical treatment. He was probably suffering from a type of Parkinson's disease which made him lose much of the movement of his arms and legs. "His face shows the mask-like rigidity usual in these cases," the university said.

Because of this, Prinz had to take early retirement. The university did, however, make him an honorary reader in German. Divorced and with no family in South Africa, he was forced to return to Germany in the middle of the war and died at Göttingen on 1 September 1942 at the age of 56.

At the time of her divorce, Irma was 39 years old. An entire phase of her life had come to an end. Having lost contact with Prinz and the German-speaking world of the university, she plunged herself into the English-speaking art world. From 1933 onwards, all her notes in her clippings book were written in English rather than German. She no longer spoke German to her brother Rudi, who had married an English-speaking wife.

In 1935 her father Samuel Stern died on his farm in Schweizer-Reneke. Henny continued to write to her daughter in German, but the last surviving letters from her in 1939 are in English, although they still begin "Dearest *Irmakind* (Irma child)" and are signed "Your *Mutter* (mother)".

By the end of World War 2, Berlin had been almost completely destroyed by bombing. After revisiting the parts of Berlin that Irma knew and had spent part of her childhood in, the British poet Stephen Spender remarked: "The contours which I saw through the darkness were torn, jagged edges, the only noises which one heard were creakings and flappings … I realised that everything was like this, that an enormous shroud of sadness had blurred and covered the whole face of Berlin and that nothing which I knew existed any longer."

Four years after the war ended, Irma herself began to take stock of how much she had changed. She resumed writing to her German friend Trude Bosse after an absence of many years. "I have buried the past; that is why I have kept silent," she wrote. "One shudders when one thinks of a country, its culture, its well-disposed people, all in a mass grave, hence my silence. Now you know. There is scarcely anything personal involved. Everything that comes from Germany is like a vanished age to me, like an echo from a sunken world."

CHAPTER 9

Suné Raubenheimer

IRMA'S BEST FRIENDS, RICHARD AND FREDA FELDMAN

Irma once revealed in the *Cape Review* that her late father had been one of her harshest critics. She said: "In my own house the revolution against my work set in. One day my father discovered that I had modelled the figure of a nude pregnant woman and without a word he flung this piece of sculpture out of the first-floor window onto the street."

In 1935, two years after she divorced her husband, Irma's father died. These two events seem to have given Irma a new sense of independence and freedom. Although she was still very attached to her mother, Henny, who moved in with her, Irma came to rely more and more on her friends for their help and support. Her two best friends were a Jewish couple, Richard and Freda Feldman. Irma often stayed with the Feldmans and their two children when she was exhibiting in Johannesburg.

Richard and Freda were so accommodating that they even cleared the dining room in their Houghton home so that Irma had a spacious studio to work in. Richard was one of Irma's most ardent admirers, collecting and helping her market her work in Johannesburg. He frequently wrote reviews of her exhibitions. In *The Zionist Record*, he wrote: "When our times are stormy, the art of the day reflects the storm. In Irma Stern's painting we find the thunder of new creation."

Irma's new-found freedom allowed her to fulfil her yearning to travel alone into Africa to paint the people and places she had dreamt of. Everything until then had been in preparation for this work, which became the high point of her career.

Irma Stern was certainly the first South African artist to undertake such trips – without knowing her final destination or the kind of people she would encounter, or even whether local tradition would allow her to paint them. For many of the people she painted, even in the rural areas of Pondoland and Swaziland, it was the first time they had met or been in close contact with a white woman. But it is clear from the hundreds of drawings and paintings she did that she was able to establish a rapport with her models which overcame the barriers of language, race, class and culture.

Between 1939 and 1949, Irma made two trips to Zanzibar and two to the Belgian Congo. She endured physical hardships, long journeys, met and painted lots of interesting people and enjoyed the challenge of visiting exotic places. She also produced many paintings, charcoal drawings and gouaches during these visits. The vibrant colours reflect the rich atmosphere of the cultures in which she immersed herself. She wrote two illustrated books about her African voyages: *Zanzibar* and *Congo*.

On 22 October 1939, Irma wrote to Richard and Freda about her first trip to Zanzibar, an island off the coast of Tanzania. She described it as "the place of gold, ebony, ivory and slaves [that] brought the Arabs to Africa. As early as the tenth century, they came to settle in Zanzibar – the island of spices."

It was a place of intense enjoyment: "Had the most fantastic time in Zanzibar – a heap of new friends – partly white, partly brown. A life so full of interest and fun – I am sorry I am back – as I find it more than dull and uncultured."

Apart from the many pictures she painted of Muslim men and women, Irma also brought back an antique door which became the imposing front door of her house, The Firs. A journalist who interviewed Irma in 1946 was overcome with wonder when he first saw it:

A door of dark mellowed wood exquisitely carved and as I knocked I felt that such a door could only open into a temple – perhaps into some place with Aladdin touches. It might easily have been a door to open the way into the atmosphere of the Arabian nights. An odd door to find in a Rosebank street, odd, too, to find it on a house called The Firs.

The imposing carved front door to The Firs, which Irma brought back from Zanzibar

Along with the door, Irma brought back a heavy, carved chest which Freda greatly admired and two high-backed red velvet armchairs which she placed in her lounge. "They accommodated her size very comfortably and made her look as if she were holding court in a sultan's palace," Mona, Freda's daughter, wrote in her book, *Remembering Irma*. "When Freda or Richard visited, she would often place one of them beside her in the matching 'royal chair' for a tête-à-tête."

Her first trip to Zanzibar in 1939 had resulted in a huge body of work that kept Irma busy for many years preparing for exhibitions. But she hated not being able to travel to Europe because of the war, so Africa became the focus of her travels.

By March 1942, she began to plan a trip to the Congo. She wrote to Richard and Freda in a letter brimming with excitement:

The Congo – I am getting all the information I can. I am getting letters of introduction also to the Belgian Congo government – I want a change badly. Here if war is at the door, what do I do, but sit and get bombed? I have no bomb to throw back! There I can at least enjoy adventure of a more primitive nature – cannibals or lions or such things, and yet paint. I now still have money to go there – maybe later I have spent it all.

There was another reason Irma was anxious to leave Cape Town. Her mother Henny had been very ill, which exhausted her. A constant stream of day and night nurses invaded The Firs. When Henny recovered, Irma knew it was time to go: she had her exit permit and her passport ready. Not even the pleas of Freda not to go could change her mind.

In her book, *Congo*, Irma wrote:

> *The Congo has always been for me the symbol of Africa, the very heart of Africa. The sound 'Congo' makes my blood dance with the thrill of excitement; it sounds to me like the distant native drums and heavy tropical river, its water floating in mystic depths… And now I am travelling through the Congo, through miles of dense forest with dry trees and grey green foliage, so many hours of it that it has a hypnotic charm. Not a living soul passes, just trees and trees, the great Congo forest.*

Watussi Woman, 1942

Usually fond of her creature comforts, Irma was prepared to rough it in the Congo. She slept in poor living conditions, ate very basic food and did not always have access to running water. It was a tough, four-month working expedition full of flies, heat, rotten meat and rough roads.

But the price was worth it – she was not only able to paint the beautiful landscape, but also the Watussi people, including the queen and other members of the royal family. "Never have I seen such beauty," wrote Irma. "It was expressive of a highly-bred, cultured, ancient race."

On 8 July 1942, she wrote to Richard and Freda:

> *Here I am in the heart of Africa… I am working very hard – but it is a great task – the heat – the sun's rays – the altitude… I am here since about ten days or so – have seen two dances of*

the Watussi... I have painted the dancers and after that, the slave musicians... Have been in the Congo five weeks... Here is another painter, Belgian, very pleasant man, but his work is smooth and sweet... It takes away a bit of the wild charm to have another artist working pretty-pretty things so near by.

Irma planned to work her way up north to Stanleyville to find the Mangbetu people, whom she had heard "only one generation back had been man-eaters". In her book, *Congo*, Irma describes how much she admired the Mangbetu:

It was strange to plunge right among so savage a tribe and yet only to be aware of a rare artistic taste... Here were the creators of magnificent pieces of sculpture carved out of wood... grotesque and beautiful... Here live men who are treated with respect due to their artistic craft.

Irma loved the Congo, despite the bad roads and unappetising food. She found the sights and sounds she encountered intensely stimulating. Her Congo paintings are among the most exciting works she ever produced – the bold colours laid on thickly with the curving strokes of her palette knife seem to leap off the canvas. Her experience of the Congo was like being in a Garden of Eden, Irma said in a letter to the Feldmans in September 1942:

At night the forest glows with swarming fire flies and a buzzing and singing begins, a dark heaving noise of frogs, the insect sounds at night like a huge orchestra. The forest is alive with animals, shy buck, monkeys and bats. Birds cry and elephants tread down the trembling, dew-covered young palms. A deep male voice calls a few sweet melodic tunes – a woman's voice answers – and a third, higher voice repeats the same sweet love call. The forest is green and luscious: the forest is endless like a green dream of Creation Day.

Irma had to return home to prepare for an exhibition of her work in Johannesburg that November. The trip to Congo had exhausted her not only physically and artistically, but financially as well, so she wrote to Richard and Freda to ask for their help in organising it.

"I do not want to spend an awful lot of money, as this trip is costing me a heck of a lot," she explained. "I hope you will help me in getting the right place."

Irma Stern at home surrounded by her antique collection, 1965

After each of her journeys, Irma added to her collection of rare artefacts and pieces of furniture from Europe and Africa. As she drove through remote villages in the Congo, her driver used to call out in the local dialect: "Bring out all your old rubbish – the mad old woman will buy it!"

One of the rare objects she bought there is a wooden stool carved in 1890 for a Luba chief. The carved figure represents a woman, as it was believed the power of the chief was handed down through his mother. In her still life of 1952, *Buli Stool with Fruit*, Irma painted the stool carrying half a melon. She liked to mix fruit, flowers and objects in her still-life compositions.

Visitors to The Firs today will see that it has been converted into a museum dedicated to the work of Irma Stern. It has been left just as it was before Irma died and many of the objects that she collected are on display, including the carved door from Zanzibar, the high-backed velvet chairs she liked to sit on and the Buli stool. They were all reminders to Irma of her travels and created a rich mix of different cultures in her own home, which she saw as a refuge.

CHAPTER 10

Suné Raubenheimer

Dudley Welch often accompanied Irma on her travels

Irma had an intense and complex relationship with her mother, Henny. Both women were strong-willed and liked to have their own way. Irma's friend Hilda described Henny as "a dove-grey battle ship in full dress."

After her father died, Henny moved in with Irma at The Firs. This must have strained their relationship. Even while Irma was married to Johannes Prinz, Henny sponsored their lavish lifestyle and paid for many of their overseas trips. This made Irma dependent on her mother, which she hated. She felt that her mother controlled her.

The fact that Henny was ill for the last two years of her life also made Irma anxious. She wrote to her friend Freda: "My life – a few days I run about in a whirl of happiness – I work and life seems full and potent to me – then a few scenes with my mother and she just is resentful that I am not ill as she is. She resents my food – my friends – my going out – just my whole me."

Their relationship was marred by frustration and anger. But when Henny was diagnosed with cancer in 1939, Irma felt sorry for her mother, describing her as "all thin and her face white and full of horror and pain." Irma often was responsible for nursing her mother back to health with the help of day and night nurses, but this prevented her from doing what she loved most: her art.

Her response to this feeling of being trapped with her sick mother was to escape. Irma went on long trips to remote destinations like Swaziland, Zanzibar and the Congo not only to paint, but to regain her sense of freedom. On one occasion Irma wrote to Freda about how she felt staying at home, "This is all one thought – how can I get away and where to – staying here means getting hard and unemotional – calculating and what for? Life to me these days is a complete misery."

To be fair, Irma was not the easiest person in the world to get along with. Naturally, she had an artistic temperament, which meant she was often self-centred, volatile and easily offended. Although Irma never admitted it, it must have been equally hard for Henny to share the house with her.

The frequent squabbles at The Firs affected both of them. Because Henny was the person closest to her, it is understandable that Irma often blamed her when things went wrong. In April 1936, Irma wrote to Richard and Freda, thanking them for hosting her on a recent trip to Johannesburg. But then she broke into another rant about her mother: "The arriving was an anti-climax. Nobody to fetch me from the train. Mother had for some mysterious reason avoided to understand that morning meant morning and not evening. Well and ever since, she has been simply beastly to me."

When her brother Rudi and his family came to visit Irma and Henny at The Firs, the tension was temporarily relieved.

Often when mother and daughter fought, Henny would threaten to cut Irma out of her will, which must have distressed Irma. Being an artist, it was difficult for her to fully support herself.

Another indication of their sometimes strained relationship was the curious incident in February 1944 when Irma mounted a huge exhibition in Cape Town. There were hundreds of people on opening night and it was her largest and most successful exhibition in the Mother City. On display was a portrait of her mother which had never been seen before.

Writing later, Irma said, "I had a rather strange interlude at my opening – with the hall filled to capacity – my mother got up and tore her portrait down – put it under her skirts and out she went – I was wild about it."

Irma could not understand why her mother objected so much to the painting, but it was probably because Henny found the portrait unflattering. It is also unlikely that Irma asked her mother's permission before putting the picture on public display.

The thing that most strikes you about the portrait of Henny is how much like Irma it is. They were both imposing, larger-than-life women. Henny's strong presence is reinforced by her double chin.

Describing the painting, Freda's daughter Mona Berman wrote, "Steely blue eyes gaze with some contempt at the viewer, while the mouth, set in a grim expression, displays little warmth and compassion, showing the sitter's distaste for posing for her portrait."

Portrait of Henny Stern, 1943

At the same time, Mona felt the painting depicted the strength and determination of the Jewish women in Germany who fled the country before World War 2, escaping Hitler's reign of terror.

The year in which the painting was done, 1943, was a difficult one for Irma. "My mother is getting ill and gradually getting worse," she wrote to Richard and Freda. "Very hard to watch it all and not to be able to do a thing."

During this emotionally draining time for Irma, she found refuge in her art. She worked very hard in her studio and went off in April to paint some seascapes. A few weeks later she complained of the mess in her home and "the atmosphere of disaster in the air."

Fortunately, there were some good things that had happened: "The finances have been discussed – so that I can look into the future with no anxiety – also the situation between my brother and myself is in order again. We are on the same good footing as when we were children and also my sister-in-law and I are getting on all right."

In September, she pushed aside her problems at The Firs to focus on her exhibition in Johannesburg, where she showed off her paintings from Congo, Zanzibar and Senegal. Knowing that Henny was "incurably ill and may die any day," Irma was glad to be back at her side after the exhibition was over. Henny died a week later.

"I was just in time," she wrote to Freda. "Mother passed away Wednesday – a week ago. She had taken a bad turn Sunday and was more or less under morphine till she died. I could just shake hands with her once more … It was a terrible shock all the same to me."

Even though they did not have a very affectionate relationship, it is clear that Irma loved her mother and mourned her loss. Three weeks after her death, she wrote, "It is only now – I am beginning to understand life and all that my mother meant to me. I am feeling horribly lonely at times … I am alone all day long."

Yet in other ways, it must have been something of a relief to Irma. She could now come and go freely and began making plans to renovate The Firs, which her mother probably would not have approved of. From now, Irma was alone – no father, no husband and no mother. Nobody to tell her what to do; she could live her life as she pleased. And that suited her just fine.

Another relationship which played a huge role in Irma's life was her friendship with Richard and Freda Feldman. Irma relied on their support, both financial and emotional, and often needed their reassurance.

The flurry of letters between Richard, Freda and Irma bear testimony to their intimate friendship. Once, when Richard and Freda had taken too long to respond to one of her letters, Irma wrote, "Are you still alive? Why do you never write to me? Do you not love me any more?"

The relationship between Irma and Freda was similar to a mother-daughter relationship, without the shadow of guilt. "For Irma, Freda was a nurturing yet undemanding presence, as well as the child and protégée that she never had," Mona wrote in her book. "In this way, their friendship was rewarding, but non-threatening to both of them."

Irma and Freda had a lot in common: they were both Jewish, they adored flowers, colour, hats and shoes, and they loved staging elaborate meals. They believed the food should look as good as it tasted.

"Freda enjoyed Irma's sense of style, her lavish lifestyle, sound knowledge and good judgement in collecting antiques and art works from all over the world," remembered Mona. "Though much younger than Irma, Freda provided her with the unconditional acceptance and nurturing that possibly was lacking in her complex relationship with her mother."

Irma posing with one of her paintings, 1946

Towards the end of her life, Irma did find a male companion with whom she got on well. His name was Dudley Welch. They became friends when Irma's mother was ill in 1944. Although they never married, he stuck loyally by her side for the next 20 years.

When World War 2 ended in 1945, Irma felt a surge of relief. "What a treat the news!" she wrote. "The world opens up again – suddenly there is a Paris and a Florence – a Rome and a world shining out of the ruins to build up..."

Indeed, the outside world did open up to Irma again. In 1947, she went on her first European trip in ten years, working in the south of France, Italy and Spain and exhibiting in Paris, London and the Netherlands. Irma's confidence grew as her work gained recognition in Europe. Several well-known galleries offered to exhibit her work.

Perhaps she was encouraged to travel to Europe by the news that came in 1947. When the British royal family was visiting South Africa, Queen Elizabeth (the present Queen's mother) bought one of her paintings! This was without a doubt the most important sale during Irma's lifetime.

When she returned to Cape Town in January 1948, she was still elated about the acclaim she had received and ready to start painting again. "My work is going ahead miles," she wrote to Freda. "I have had very good press in Holland – they talk of a God-sent talent..."

This happiness Irma felt about her art and life coincided with the start of her relationship with Dudley. He was an architect whom Irma had met at one of her exhibitions in Durban in 1935. They met again in 1939 when Dudley joined a firm of architects in Cape Town.

When he was writing his thesis at UCT, he often visited Irma at The Firs. Right from the beginning, there was a spark of romance between Irma and Dudley, although Henny did not approve of him. "Mother is shouting the place down that Welch is a leech and a sponge. I wish somehow this would stop to give peace," Irma confided to Freda.

Afraid of getting hurt again, Irma preferred to call him "Welch" rather than by his first name. Later on, when he became a permanent fixture in her life, she reverted to the more affectionate "Dudley", even signing her letters and Christmas cards from both of them. In the 1950s and 1960s, Irma came to rely on Dudley more and more. He was not only the person who took care of her house, but also a treasured companion.

"In spite of local gossip that he was around only for the material benefits, Irma's volatile personality and egocentric behaviour would have made it impossible for Dudley to remain at her side for 22 years had he not cared deeply about her," wrote Mona Berman in *Remembering Irma*. "Nor would Irma have been able to tolerate Dudley's ponderous, small-minded and at times abrasive personality had she not been fond of him and sincerely valued his presence in her life. But nowhere in her letters is there any indication that either Irma or Dudley wanted to marry the other."

Perhaps one of the reasons they never married was because Irma was Jewish and Dudley was Catholic. Or maybe he was put off by the fact that she was a divorcee. The more likely reason is that Irma was fiercely independent and did not want any legal attachment to him. When she died, he inherited very little.

Even so, she could not have done without Dudley's help. From the time he entered her life, Dudley took on more and more of the difficult jobs that Irma was unable to handle: arranging exhibitions, getting paintings framed and transporting them to galleries. He helped with the catalogues, invitations and the sale of her work.

Towards the end of her life, when Irma's health was failing and she was very obese, she could not have travelled alone. Dudley did all the hotel bookings, drove their hired car and ensured that Irma had all the creature comforts she needed. This included going to the theatre and to concerts together, which they both enjoyed.

Irma was passionate about Africa, but she was not particularly politically minded. In 1958, Irma was asked to give one of her paintings to support Nelson Mandela and others in the Treason Trial. Although she did so, she confessed in a letter to Freda: "I don't particularly want to be mixed up more in this business."

Two years later, when she was visiting Europe, Irma's health began to deteriorate rapidly. She had diabetes, a disease which results in high blood sugar, as well as heart and lung problems.

Nevertheless, she was shocked to learn how bad it was:

> *I have been anything but well – I knew I was ill – but had no idea how seriously ill I was till I found a very good specialist in [Switzerland] and have been living with a strict diet and tons*

of medicine ever since I got here. I am so-called better, but very run down still.

By February 1961, Irma still had health problems, writing to Freda of a bout of flu. She and Dudley were in Spain, where Irma was enjoying a measure of fame: "I am hard at work. Am doing work that astonishes even me – the local press has lately discovered me and simply put articles out 'La Picasso' [the female Picasso] – the multi-millionairess etc… So you see, wherever I go, I still cause a bit of an uproar."

Sadly, at the very point in her life when she was so self-assured and her art had won wide acclaim, Irma was hampered by poor health. It must have been very hard for her. On arriving back at The Firs after her travels abroad, getting down to work again took a long time. "Am slowly starting again – it is a delicate flower – art – and so dead when not treated rightly," she wrote to Richard and Freda.

Throughout her life, Irma maintained the practice of making sketches before she started to paint. Wherever she travelled, she would take notes of what the people looked like and what colours were around her. These rough sketches, usually in ink, gouache or pastel, helped her remember landscapes and subjects when she returned to her studio to paint.

By the 1960s, Irma no longer used the thick impasto paint she had once been so fond of. Instead she started her paintings in diluted colour. Over this, in light brush strokes, she would paint layers of thin paint in bright colours. Sometimes she scribbled on her paintings to add texture and movement.

No longer primarily concerned with Africa, her subject matter was more universal now, including landscapes, still lifes and European scenes, such as *Pimento Harvest* of 1962. This painting uses intense complementary colours of red for the tomatoes and green for the hills. Workers and nature appear to be in harmony.

I am in a state of nervous collapse – just think what has happened to me? Out of the blue I got an invitation to have a retrospective show in one of London's best galleries this year – 40 oils and a lot of drawings – I am so overwhelmed that I can't do a damn thing! No charges – fully insured – freight and all – catalogues, invitations – all free. If this is a success, I am made.

THE WALL OF PORTRAITS IN THE IRMA STERN MUSEUM

The invitation had come from the Grosvenor Gallery for an exhibition in November. It promised to seal her reputation as a world-class artist, but sadly it never took place. Irma did, however, receive recognition before she died. Apart from the Medal of Honour for Art awarded to her by the Oppenheimer Trust, she received a gold medal from the *Suid-Afrikaanse Akademie vir Wetenskap en Kuns* (the South African Academy of Science and Arts).

"They waited too long to give me a thrill," she joked in a letter. It was not entirely a happy occasion. Irma was cross that the speech made at the ceremony mentioned Maggie Laubser, a famous local artist, whom Irma did not rate very highly. She was also upset that Richard and Freda could not be there to share the occasion with her.

By May, Irma was very ill. She must have realised how unlikely it was that the London exhibition would go ahead. "I have been in bed for the last five weeks," she told Freda. "Ill – neuritis of legs from diabetes – painful like anything." This left her legs feeling tingly and numb.

An example of a picture study Irma did in Cannes, 1957

In another letter, she spoke of the two doctors who attended her, her day and night nurse and the attention that Dudley gave her. She was now in almost the same position her mother had been in 23 years earlier, bedridden and helpless.

"I am having a most awful time," she complained. "I suppose everybody is doing all they can to help me – I am full of pain. My legs look like elephantism and are full of water – swollen – hard."

By July she was well enough to receive guests for tea in her studio, but was unable to leave The Firs. "I am very displeased at my state of health," she wrote. "Have lost 20 pounds (9kg) and look like a hag... My one leg is still open and oozes water, so I cannot go out."

Shortly before Irma died, Freda and Richard had to cancel their holiday in Cape Town due to Richard's poor health. On the morning of 23 August 1966, they received two telegrams from Dudley that Irma was critically ill at Volks Hospital (now known as Cape Town Medi-Clinic in Gardens). Late that night came another telegram: "Deeply regret Irma passed away tonight." She had died due to heart failure, ending her long struggle with diabetes. Freda and Richard were devastated that they had not been able to see her one last time.

Dudley wrote to them, describing the end of her life:

> *Although Irma's death was not unexpected, it was a great shock. I had always hoped she would get better. The doctor in [France] gave her 18 months and she had 17 of them. The last night she had started drawing in the special nurses' notebook and I recognised them as the continuous-type drawings in ink which were the kind she always started her work period with. She'd been looking at a book of African paintings and she had just given a reply to me, 'I will get better'... and then she died.*

When Irma's will was read out, Dudley and Freda discovered that The Firs was to be sold, a thought which appalled Freda. She insisted that the house be preserved as a museum. "She involved all her family and friends, and contacted whoever she thought might be of assistance," remembered Mona Berman. "She wrote letters to the City Council, to the mayor, the daily newspapers in Cape Town and Johannesburg... and others."

On 11 October, Freda's plea was published in *The Star*:

> *As a very old friend of hers since 1931, and as one who knew her as few people did, I would like to add my strong recommendation*

to those in charge of her estate to preserve her home as an Irma Stern Museum. Apart from her own works, she has over the many years during her travels collected antiques and unique objets d'art which were in themselves an expression of her personality. This collection is one of the most valuable in this country and would lend itself admirably to an appropriate museum of this great South African artist.

The executors of Irma's estate took a long time to make up their minds, arguing that the house was not easy to find and that it was in poor condition and a security risk. Some suggested that Irma's art collection be moved to a special gallery in Cape Town or Johannesburg. But in the end, Freda and Dudley's efforts paid off. On 12 January 1967, Dudley sent Freda this telegram, "The Firs to become an Irma Stern Museum. Love Dudley."

After months of uncertainty, it had at last been decided that Irma's house would become a museum administered by the University of Cape Town and kept exactly as it was – the studio with its pungent smell of paint and jars of brushes, the beautiful Spanish medieval table in her dining room, the unique African sculptures and the "majestic armchairs in which Irma Stern sat as a reigning queen," just as Freda and other friends remembered them. It was a great victory. Freda sent this telegram in reply, "Congratulations – exciting news, Irma's Museum – Love Freda."

Apart from the museum commemorating her work, Irma's lasting legacy is her art. She liked to listen to classical music while she painted, especially Beethoven and Bach, and as a child she had wanted to become a dancer. This love of music and movement is reflected in her paintings. The brush strokes sing over the canvas in a swirl of movement.

Irma loved colour, too, and was not afraid to use bold colours that sometimes clashed loudly. At other times, the colours are soft and soothing. Her still lifes, such as *Flowers and Fruit* of 1937, are a reminder of the objects that Irma loved so much, like an antique vase, her appreciation of flowers, as well as the fruit she enjoyed eating once she'd finished painting.

The artist that Irma most admired when it came to still lifes was Cézanne. She often wished she could paint fruit as well as he could. As for flowers, they were a source of joy to Irma and she continued to paint them throughout her life. Once when she bumped into the sculptor, Jacob

Epstein, in London in 1938, she was gratified with the high praise he gave her art. "Renoir's roses look like paper next to yours," he gushed.

If you visit the Irma Stern Museum today, tucked away in Rosebank in the shadow of Table Mountain, be sure to make your way to the red wall in the sitting room covered in portraits. It was here that Irma really excelled as an artist: she had a gift for seeing her subjects as they really were, revealing what lay beneath the surface.

Mona Berman described a portrait that Irma did of her aunt Mary who was beautiful, but the picture shows a troubled soul, weighed down by sadness and disappointment. "It seemed uncanny, as if Irma had looked right into her core and exposed the inner torment that Mary kept so well concealed from the rest of us," Mona wrote.

Her portraits did not always meet with approval: why else did her friend Roza van Gelderen hide a portrait that Irma had painted of her under her bed for so many years? Roza found the portrait hideous.

When painting portraits, Irma didn't mind what the model wore, but she was very fussy about the quality of the light. She would stare intently at the model and then step back with half-closed eyes. She aimed to finish her portraits in one sitting.

Much of the work of composing a painting took place in her mind first. "I work a long time at a picture in my head," she told the *Rand Daily Mail* in 1964. "I never touch the canvas after it is finished."

Although she did not have strong spiritual beliefs, Irma was drawn to religious subjects. She painted many pictures of Christian scenes, such as the angel Gabriel announcing the news of Jesus' birth to Mary and Mary posing with the infant Messiah. No doubt she found the very act of creating a kind of spiritual fulfilment in itself. She believed that art should have a positive influence on the world and that it should be "strength-giving and wholesome".

Today, Irma has finally achieved the lasting international recognition she had always wanted and is known as one of South Africa's greatest artists. The prices that her paintings earn at auctions are a clear indication of this. In 2014, *Zanzibar Woman* fetched over R18,5 million, while the year before *Malay Bride* went for R20,7 million. But the highest price ever paid for one of her paintings was a whopping R52,5 million, which was given for *Arab Priest* in 2011 by the Qatar Orientalist Museum.

What would Irma have thought of how much people spend today on her paintings? Perhaps she would have found it ridiculous. While she was alive, she was happy to receive a few hundred rand for one of her works. But she undoubtedly knew that she possessed a great talent and from the time she was a young girl living in the dry veld of Schweizer-Reneke to the moment she died in Cape Town, she had explored it to the full.

Speaking of Irma, Richard Feldman wrote: "It is given to very few to see the true soul of things." Looking at the wall of portraits in the Irma Stern Museum, you understand just how much and how fully Irma really saw.

Portrait of Mary Kramer, 1941

BIBLIOGRAPHY

1. Arnold, M. *Irma Stern: A Feast for the Eye.* Rembrandt van Rijn Art Foundation, Fernwood Press. Vlaeberg, 1995.
2. Berman, M. *Remembering Irma.* Double Storey Books, Cape Town, 2003.
3. Schoeman, K. *Irma Stern: the Early Years, 1894–1933.* National Library of South Africa, Cape Town, 1994.
4. Smuts, H. *Reflections of a Journey: An Educational Resource.* Standard Bank Studio, Johannesburg, 2003.
5. Smuts, H. *At Home with Irma Stern.* UCT Irma Stern Museum and the Irma Stern Trust, Cape Town, 2007.

Portrait of Freda Feldman in Basuto Hat, 1943

ABOUT THIS BOOK

The Story of Irma Stern is intended to be the first in a series of books for children telling the life stories of influential South Africans. The book was commissioned by Susan Keegan, a director of The Vine School in Cape Town. The school follows the rich, literature-based Ambleside curriculum, which includes studying the lives and works of great men and women. As with many curricula developed in Europe or America, the focus tends to be on those who shaped Western art and culture. Susan has long recognised the inspirational value of stories about local people, but she was unable to find substantial biographies written for young readers about African artists, musicians, inventors and explorers.

In 2014 a generous gift was given to the school to be used at Susan's discretion. She decided to use it to research and publish a children's book about a famous South African artist. Then she found out that Katherine Graham, a parent of two boys at The Vine School, is a children's author. They met, discovered a shared appreciation for the inspirational power of stories, and so the journey began.

With so many great South Africans to choose from, they struggled to select the first candidate. In the end, they settled on Irma Stern because pupils at the school would be able to visit the Irma Stern Museum, conveniently situated nearby in Rosebank. There they could view many of Irma's own artworks, study her collection of African art and artefacts, and picture the artist herself living and working in The Firs below the University of Cape Town. Although they hoped the book would be of interest to many others, their first intention was to write a biography that would inspire the children of The Vine School.

The book you now hold in your hands took two years to complete. Many hours of research, writing, editing, illustrating and sourcing images have been poured into this project. We hope you enjoy learning about the life of one of South Africa's greatest artists. May you be inspired, as Irma Stern was, to find beauty in the world around you and create your own masterpieces.